TIFFANY
windows

TIFFANY windows

ALASTAIR DUNCAN

with 230 illustrations, 114 in color

SIMON AND SCHUSTER · NEW YORK

TO ALICE

(*Frontispiece*)
Two panels from the Strong Memorial window in the First Presbyterian Church, Albany, New York. (See color plate 66.)

Copyright © 1980 by Alastair Duncan
All rights reserved including the right of
reproduction in whole or in part in any form.
This 1982 edition is published by Bookthrift
A Simon and Schuster Division of Gulf and Western Corporation
by arrangement with Thames and Hudson, Ltd., London
Simon and Schuster Building
Rockefeller Center
1230 Avenue of the Americas
New York, New York 10020
Bookthrift is a registered trademark of Simon and Schuster
New York, New York

1 2 3 4 5 6 7 8 9 10

Library of Congress Cataloging in Publication Data

Duncan, Alastair, date.
  Tiffany windows.

  Bibliography: p.
  Includes index.
    1. Tiffany, Louis Comfort, 1848–1933. 2. Glass
painting and staining – – United States. I. Title.
NK5398.T52D86   748.5913   80-5352
ISBN 0-89673-147-2

Printed and bound in Italy by Arnoldo Mondadori, Verona

Contents

Acknowledgments

THIS BOOK is as much a tribute to modern photography as it is to Tiffany. Very special thanks go to Elton Schnellbacher, who travelled throughout America to photograph the vast majority of the windows pictured in these pages. Others include Lehland Cook, Kenneth Hay, William Paulus, Edward Jacoby, James Clark, Sanders Milens, Dennis McWaters, Ralph Pyle, Beverly Hall, Lawrence Orlick, Erig Borg, Timothy Osner, Erne Frueh, Gordon Smith, Studio One in Plymouth, Mass., Michael Friedlander and, finally, the team of Christie's photographers under Vincent Miraglia.

Gratitude is also extended to those who helped in the research; in particular, Gordon Henderson, Fred and Nancy Dikeman, Lillian Nassau, Professor Robert Koch, Frederick Brandt, Norman Rice, Joseph Levi, Dr. Martin Ruddock, Jane Farver, Henry Hawley, Virginia Hyvarinen, Rita Reif, Susan Johnson, Sona Johnston, Bruce Berrian, Beryl Tumpson, and Henry Fruhauf.

Introduction

IT IS DIFFICULT for us today to appreciate the enthusiasm of the 1890s for American stained glass windows because we have rejected this form of architectural decoration almost completely. We must, therefore, gauge Tiffany's work in the light of the then all-pervasive fashion for these windows, a fashion largely inspired by Tiffany himself. We should, furthermore, see it in the context of the wider concern of artists and architects of that time for the applied arts in general, a concern nurtured by the exhortations of the Arts and Crafts movement for a fresh start.

To comprehend fully Tiffany's revolutionary contribution to, and eventual monolithic influence on, the stained glass of the period one must go back five hundred years to the craft's forgotten highpoint.

The windows of the fourteenth century were comprised of mosaics of broken color. The glass was a type of "pot metal" in which the color permeated the entire mass. It was handmade in unequal thicknesses and filled with air bubbles and other imperfections which added greatly to its brilliance by affording many points against which the sun's rays were broken. The pieces of glass were small and put together with broad leads, which together provided the mosaic effect. Later, this concept was almost completely abandoned. Stained glass artists introduced large pieces of glass into their windows on which they painted their saint lore, brushing on liberal amounts of stain and enamel to provide the detail. The effect was weak and dull, resembling a picture on glass instead of canvas. The color was no longer *in* the glass, but now *on* it in the form of opaque paints which interfered with the material's translucency.

Sir Joshua Reynolds was one of many celebrated painters to misunderstand the medium. As he himself explained, "I had frequently pleased myself with reflecting, after I had produced what I thought a brilliant effect of light and shadow on my canvas, how greatly that effect would be heightened by the transparency which the painting on glass would be sure to produce. It turned out quite the reverse."

By 1800 the craft had reached its lowest point. The glorious reds and blues of the Gothic cathedrals had long since gone, replaced by endless, dreary, painted definition described by one disenchanted critic as "lamentably unglasslike . . . a studious, slavish, uninspired imitation of antique work in which even the dirt is imitated!"

In America, the stained glass artist found himself in a multiple impasse. Not only did the churches in the United States commission their stained glass memorials from England and Europe, thereby depriving him of work, but this work for which he was passed over was of such inferior quality. Nor could he, in effect, compete on his own terms. Only a small amount of glass was manufactured in America, leaving him with no choice but to import the very material which he despised; though now it was even worse, as his counterparts overseas culled the best from each batch before it was shipped.

Clearly, the ground was laid for an American revolution.

The first matter to redress was the lack of quality glass; the second was to go back to the fourteenth century basics, to learn the art of glass anew and adapt it to modern design principles. To these ends the medium's preeminent artists now turned their energies. New formulae for pot metal glass were developed and new kilns built. Progress was fraught with pitfalls and often accidental! As Will Low, a stained glass artist who later joined Tiffany Studios, wrote in 1888, "many were the paths diligently followed only to find that they ended in quagmires, before this uniformity of excellence, worthy to be classed as a school, was reached . . ."

Two leaders in research and experimentation emerged: John La Farge and Louis C. Tiffany. Both, not surprisingly, were accomplished painters known essentially as colorists. The quality of glass was greatly improved upon. Rich, glowing colors were developed in varying degrees of translucency, often blended together in whiplash patterns which swept across each sheet. Soon afterwards came the invention of "opalescent" glass, a variety not, in fact, totally opaque, but semi-translucent. It remains a quintessential American phenomenon, one that today still distinguishes American windows from those made elsewhere.

Others to join La Farge and Tiffany in this break with tradition were Maitland Armstrong, Henry Crowninshield, Otto Heinigke, Frederick Lamb, and Florence Tillinghast. The movement became known as the American School of Stained Glass, whose philosophy was simple: a window's definition should be contained as much as possible within the glass itself. The only painted detail allowed was for the face and hands in figure windows.

Tiffany could not have achieved what he did at any other point in time. His career in stained glass coincided with the enormous religious fervor which swept the United States in the 1870s. In 1875 alone over 4,000 churches of all denominations were under construction, each to be proudly embellished with memorials to former cherished members of the congregation and clergy. In the secular world, construction kept pace. The towns which had sprung up along the railroads linking the two coasts had grown into cities as the population increased and shifted westwards. New colleges, libraries, and state capitols had to be both built and decorated. Great fortunes were amassed in lumber, coal, steel, and transportation, fortunes which allowed for opulent life-styles and homes.

Decorative windows became highly fashionable as a form of domestic decoration. Charles Cole wrote in 1879 that stained glass windows could be seen "on every side of the city," in apartments, shops, railroad stations, and even steamships. Ten years later Samuel Bing wrote that "there is scarcely a respectable house today whose entrance does not boast a stained glass overdoor. Further, this colored glass is frequently seen filling the curve of archways between two sitting rooms." The new School had established itself. It remained only for its members to vie amongst themselves for the commissions which poured in.

From the start, Tiffany's greatest adversary was La Farge. A lengthy critical analysis of their respective talents and innovations exceeds the scope of this book, but brief mention must be made of La Farge's pioneership of this American stained glass revival and, thereby, of his influence on Tiffany.

A survey of articles by stained glass artists and critics in the last twenty years of the nineteenth century shows the deference paid to La Farge at that time. In every instance he is credited with initiating the revolutionary techniques which were to become the charter of the American School. Two points should be clarified from the start concerning his relationship with Tiffany. First, they *never* worked together, despite the fact that they experimented simultaneously at both the Thill and Heidt glasshouses in Brooklyn from the late 1870s. Second, it was La Farge who first incorporated opalescent glass into his windows. On completion of his first opalescent window commission (for a Dr. Richard H. Derby), La Farge immediately applied for a patent for a "Colored Glass Window" on November 10th, 1879. This was granted on February 24th, 1880. Tiffany's two patents for variations on the same opalescent techniques were granted on November 25th, 1880. The intervening months, although seemingly a small amount of time, proved a significant period in the light of the rapid technical evolutions then under way. Tiffany apparently persuaded La Farge to waive his patent with certain promises of future collaboration and, even, partnership. La Farge, naive about the commercial ramifications of this sleight-of-hand, forfeited the protection which his patent would have provided. Competition between the two became increasingly fierce and whatever mutual respect and friendship had existed earlier deteriorated rapidly.

Tiffany's subsequent meteoric success, publicized to the full by his association with the family's renowned silver firm and boundless wealth, strained the relationship still further. La Farge's resentment intensified as time passed. Tiffany not only won the commission to decorate the Lyceum Theatre, New York, by underbidding him in 1884, but he gained the favor of Stanford White and received a number of commissions from La Farge's erstwhile supporter beginning in 1888. La Farge, the single artist, could compete less and less with the enormous resources of manpower and materials which Tiffany was assembling. By the 1890s Tiffany's Glass & Decorating Company had become a juggernaut which swept most, if not all, competition aside.

Today's window enthusiast is less concerned with battles over precedence than with beauty, however, so it is fortunate that many of La Farge's greatest works have survived to bear witness to his considerable talent.

Competition did not end with La Farge. The five New York boroughs alone boasted six other major stained glass studios at the turn of the century: Frederick Lamb, Heinigke & Bowen, Heuser & Hausleiter, Charles S. Allen, H. W. Young, and Francis Lathrop. Elsewhere there was William Willet in Philadelphia, Harry E. Goodhue and Charles Connick in Boston, and Healy & Millet in Chicago. There is even a window in the Second Reformed Church in Hackensack by the glass lampshade manufacturers, Duffner & Kimberly. Tiffany maintained the lion's share through many years, but an occasional prized commission slipped by.

From the 1870s, the indefatigable Tiffany experimented against unfortunate odds in two glasshouses of his own which burned and in two others where he rented kilns. Only when the glasshouse at Corona was established in 1893 could he proceed with his tests unheeded. Kilns and chemistry were interchanged almost recklessly as the odyssey continued and finally narrowed. To the basic ingredients of glass – sand, lime, and soda – he added standard metallic oxides such as chromium, cobalt, silver, gold, and uranium in complex untried combinations. Each batch of glass was rolled flat and scientifically tested. Proven mixes and temperatures became closely guarded formulae. The search was for blended colors and textures in infinite variety and varying degrees of translucency. Even the vagaries of the melting pot – bubbles and blemishes – were harnessed in this pursuit of beauty.

These early years were primed with the uncertainty and excitement of the hunt. An English critic, Cecilia Waern, on a visit in 1897, described the back stairway at Tiffany Studios as the inner sanctum where choice pieces of glass were strewn amongst odds and ends of all kinds awaiting the attention of Mr. Tiffany or an aide; everywhere there was evidence of new departures and frank failures.

Many years later Tiffany reminisced on these formative years: "My chemist and furnace men insisted for a long time that it was impossible to achieve the results we were striving for, claiming that the metallic oxides would not combine. That was the trouble for many years. The mix would disintegrate. New style firing ovens had to be built and new methods devised for annealing glass . . . it took me thirty years to learn the art."

It also took him to England and Europe to abduct the industry's foremost glassblowers and chemists from such glass strongholds as Stourbridge and Venice. No price was too high, no competitor's wrath too great, to put paid to such epoch-making experimentation. It transcended all human considerations. In the end Tiffany stepped through and beyond the doors which had been hitherto closed to glassworkers. There was no color or texture which he finally could not make.

Yet it must be mentioned that his earliest windows were comprised entirely of glass purchased from nearby glasshouses such as Leo Popper, Dannenhoffer, Heidt, and

Thill and even from as far afield as Kokomo in Indiana. As his own experiments progressed, the percentage of non-Tiffany glass declined accordingly. By the mid-1890s he was totally independent, although continuing to purchase various "filler" varieties of glass from outside suppliers for many years when this proved cheaper than using one of his own kilns for such lower quality glass.

Numerous aspects of Tiffany's work defy comprehension, even by today's standards. For a start, the volume. There are literally *thousands* of his windows throughout the United States, many tucked quietly away in towns as remote as Ypsilanti in Michigan and Yazoo City in Mississippi. Even allowing for the fact that Tiffany's business spanned fifty years, the quantity is astounding. The commission did not end with the completed window, either. It had afterwards to be transported (those for the West Coast being shipped through Panama) and installed by a team of technicians supplemented, where necessary, by local labor. An adjoining cabinet shop at the Studios produced the wooden frames in which the windows were housed. These were often elaborate Gothic structures with ornately carved arched traceries, mullions, and spandrels. Dozens of commissions were in operation simultaneously, each closely monitored by a designer on its path through the workshops.

Today the public associates Tiffany primarily with lamps, yet the Studios' Lamp Shop evolved in the 1890s from the excess glass that had accumulated during many years of window production. The decision to manufacture lamps was a commercial one: to utilize the offcuts of glass which had been too small to incorporate into windows. Tiffany's first artistic love was always his windows; the lamps' huge later popularity helped to subsidize this love after 1900 when churches fell on bad times.

The vast majority of the firm's work was ecclesiastical. Its growth coincided with, and came, finally, to depend upon, the feverish religious activity in the United States in the late 1800s. Congregationalists, Presbyterians, Universalists, Masons, Mormons, Catholics, Baptists . . . all were building bigger and better churches and temples with which to compete for the growing number of recruits. Tiffany's importance placed him above the fray; there is scarcely a denomination which did not commission from him something on behalf of a relative or friend of the deceased. If a window was too expensive or somehow inappropriate, then a bronze or mosaic memorial tablet might prove more suitable. The Studios' Ecclesiastical Department manufactured a complete line of liturgical furnishings to supplement their windows, including crypts, altars, retables, ciboriums, and even *prie-dieux*. A Tiffany interior is an impressive sight with all the fixtures set off against white Connemara marble walls inlaid with bands of multi-colored mosaic *tesserae*. Among the major integrated Tiffany examples that have survived are St. Paul's Episcopal Church, Troy, New York; St. Michael's, New York City; the Unity Church, North Adams, Mass.; and St. Peter's Chapel, Mare Island, California. Among the most charming are St. Andrew's Dune-by-the-Sea Church in Southampton, Long Island, and the Emmanuel Episcopal Church in Dublin, New Hampshire.

Sometimes Tiffany's self-confidence exceeded the bounds of good taste. Only someone with his bravado and sense of divine mission could walk into a church in which *all* the existing windows were medieval or *grisaille* in style and be able to convince the minister (and no doubt himself, at the same time) that no other window but *his* would do for the commission at hand. Examples of inharmony abound; the Christ Episcopal Church in Fitchburg, Mass.; St. Luke's Episcopal Church in East Greenwich, Rhode Island; and St. John's in North Adams, Mass., to cite only a few. Later commissions have often added to the discord.

1   A wisteria transom showing
two characteristics of Tiffany
windows: a deeply mottled
glass for the blossoms and leaves
and a fractured, or "confetti,"
variety for the background.

2   A detail of a floral window
which also incorporates both the
mottled and "fractured" types
of glass. The latter is used in
this instance to give the
impression of looking through
dense foliage.

3 This highly important domestic window was designed by Tiffany and exhibited at the 1893 Columbian Exposition. It is illustrated in *Objects at the 1893 Chicago exposition; a synopsis . . .*, Tiffany booklet, 1893, p. 5. The text explains that the effect was "obtained without the assistance of paints or enamels." For many years seemingly forgotten on a back-porch, the window is now in a private collection.

4 The Minne-ha-ha Window designed by Mrs. Anne Weston from Duluth and displayed in the Minnesota Building at the 1893 Columbian Exposition in Chicago. It was subsequently purchased by the St. Louis County Women's Auxiliary at the Fair and presented to the Duluth Public Library, then located in the old Masonic Temple Building. The window's theme is taken from Longfellow's *Hiawatha* and shows the Indian maiden standing in front of the laughing waterfall after which she was named.

6   "Baptism of Christ," designed by Frank Brangwyn and
exhibited by Tiffany at the Grafton Galleries in 1899 (see
Dekorative Kunst, 1899, p. 122). The window was never sold, and
remained in the Tiffany Studios' stock when the firm went into
receivership in 1933. Mr. Herman Cohen, one of the liquidators,
retained the window and donated it to the Baltimore Museum of
Art. The original cartoon is illustrated in *The Decorative Art of
Frank Brangwyn*, London 1924, p. 192.

5   "Consummation of the Divine Promise in the Passing of the
Goal from the Earthly Abode to the Heavenly Home," designed by
Tiffany and installed at the entrance to the United States Pavilion at
the 1900 World Exposition in Paris. It is now in the Jeptha H.
Wade Memorial Chapel in Lakeview Cemetery, Cleveland. A
booklet published on the Chapel describes the design of the
window: "in the lower portion, an open tomb in a dark foreground
typifying the sorrows of life that end in death. About it a luxuriant
growth of poppies, the emblem of sleep, and lilies, a symbol of
resurrection, voice the hope of immortality that extends beyond
the grave."

◁7　"Christ Leaving the Praetorium," the Kempner Memorial in St. Paul's Episcopal Church, Milwaukee. Donated in 1888 by Mrs. E. H. Brodhead in memory of Wisconsin's first bishop, the window is a reproduction of Gustave Doré's painting which hung in the Doré gallery in London from 1872 to 1892. The Praetorium, to the rear, is modelled after St. George's, Hanover Square, London. Near Christ is His chief accuser, Caiaphas, the high priest. The window is not only Tiffany's largest, but incorporates more painting than any other. The central panel was later reproduced and installed in St. Mark's Episcopal Church, Washington, D.C., as the Lander Memorial.

8　"Madonna," the Bradbury Memorial in the First Congregational Church, Augusta, Maine.

9　"Truth," the Jane Ross Reynolds Memorial window in the First Presbyterian Church, Kittanning, Pa. It was illustrated in a booklet published by the Ecclesiastical Department of Tiffany's in 1913 as an example of a figure window, although it is the geometric concentration of turtle-back tiles and jewels at the top which makes it so unusual.

10 "The Four Elements," the Horsford Memorial in the Shephard Memorial Church (now the First Church Congregational), Cambridge, Mass., *c.* 1896. There is a similar set of windows in the Second Reformed Church, Hackensack, New Jersey, in memory of Martha Anderson Brown.

11 "Moses in the Bulrushes," the Arthur Ransom Law Memorial in the Congregational Church, Briarcliff Manor, New York, 1899. The same Old Testament theme was utilized in the Duncan Memorial "Moses in the Burning Bush" in the Trinity Episcopal Church, Yazoo City, Mississippi.

12 "Te Deum," the Warren Memorial in the Christ Episcopal ▷ Church, Rochester, New York, designed by Frederick Wilson, *c.* 1900. Prophets, Apostles, Martyrs, and Saints stand beneath the figure of Christ.

13 "Christ Blessing Little Children," the Amelia and Foster Barrett Memorial in Christ Episcopal Church, Greenwich, Connecticut, c. 1900. Of the dozens of windows executed by the Studios on this theme, this one appears to be the most effective.

14 "Come unto Me," the Widener Memorial in St. Stephen's Church, Philadelphia, Pa.

15 "Saint Catherine of Alexandria," the Martha Theresa Fiske Memorial installed in the Shepard Memorial Church (now the First Church Congregational), Cambridge, Mass., c. 1907.

16 "The Prophets," the Jacob and James Schwartz ▷ Memorial window in the Third Presbyterian Church, Pittsburgh. Dedicated in 1902, it represents, from the left, the Old Testament prophets, Isaiah, Jeremiah, Moses, Abraham, Ezekiel, and Daniel. A letter from Tiffany Studios in the Church's possession explains Ezekiel's appearance ". . . clean shaven because of the fifth chapter of Ezekiel, 1st verse, which reads 'and thou, son of man, take a sharp knife, take thou a barber's razor, and cause it to pass upon thy head and upon thy beard . . .' "

◁ 17   "Sacrifice of Isaac," the Daniel Bushnell Memorial window
in the East transept in the Third Presbyterian Church, Pittsburgh.
Commissioned by Bushnell's children, the window depicts
Abraham offering Isaac (*Genesis* XXII, 1–12).

18   "King Solomon," the Joseph Edward Simmons Memorial,
1911 (private collection).

19   "Nativity," the Griffith Memorial in the Christ Episcopal
Church, Rochester, New York.

20 "The River of the Water of Life," the March Memorial in St. Paul's Episcopal Church, Paterson, New Jersey. The window, considered one of Tiffany's most successful ecclesiastical commissions, was illustrated in the Studios' 1913 booklet, *Memorials in Glass and Stone*.

21 "King Solomon," a Memorial window, 1908 (private collection). The theme is taken from *I Kings* IX, 11: "Now Hiram the king of Tyre had furnished Solomon with cedar trees and fir trees, and with gold, according to all his desire."

22 The Frank Dickinson Bartlett window at the ▷ University of Chicago, 1904. Designed by Edward Sperry, it depicts a scene from Sir Walter Scott's *Ivanhoe*. Ivanhoe, having won the tournament, receives the victor's crown from Rowena. To their left are Prince John's soldiers and above is the town of Ashby de la Zouche.

23 "Gutenberg Taking the First Impression from a Movable Type Press," the Morrisson Memorial in the Morrisson-Reeves Library in Richmond, Indiana. The window was commissioned by 1895 when the library, founded by Robert Morrisson in 1864, was enlarged. Flanking panels contain the typographical symbols of other early printers: Caxton, Manutius, Vostre, and Plantin. An identical window in the Public Library in Winchester, Mass., is illustrated in *Memorials in Glass and Stone*, Ecclesiastical Department, 1913.

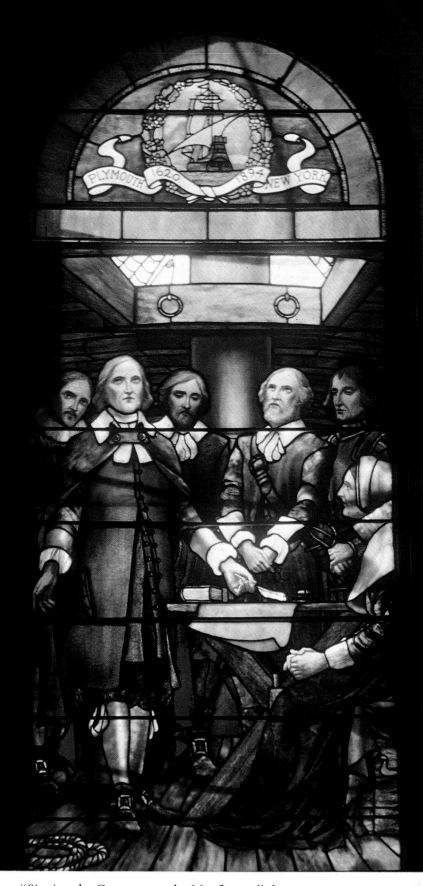

24 "Signing the Compact on the Mayflower," the Pilgrims' Memorial in the Congregational Church, Plymouth, Mass., 1894, depicting the colony's early administrators: Bradford, Miles Standish, Governor and Mrs. Carver, Brewster and Winslow. The window, in the chancel, is flanked by panels of Oliver Cromwell and John Milton, whose energies brought civil and religious liberties to England.

25 "The House of Aldus," designed by Frederick Wilson and installed in the library erected by Mary E. Hart in Troy, New York, in memory of her husband, William Howard Hart, in 1897. The window depicts Aldus Manutius in his Venetian printing house in 1502 examining a page proof of the first book, his volume of Dante's works. Also shown are his patron, Alberto Pio, Alberto Francia, who engraved the type, Peter Bembo, who edited the work, and several patricians, headed by the Doge, Leonardo Loredano. The border includes the Venetian coat-of-arms and early printers' marks.

26 "Education," presented in 1899 by Simeon Baldwin Chittenden to the Chittenden Library at Yale in memory of his daughter Mary Hartwell Lusk. The library is now a classroom.

TO
...THE HEAVY·BVRDENS
·AND·TO
...ET·THE·OPPRESSED·GO
FREE

27 "Saint George
Slaying the Dragon,"
the Memorial window
to the sailors and
soldiers who died in the
Spanish-American War,
1898, in the
Congregational Church,
Briarcliff Manor, New
York.

Tiffany played court to the period's celebrities. Following an early commission to decorate the White House under President Arthur, others quickly followed. From the Smithsonian Institution, which commissioned a series of ornamental windows, to the Hoboken Line, which ordered panels to enhance the ferry boats that plied the Hudson River between New Jersey and Manhattan, everyone sought his services.

The new class of robber barons, in particular, flocked to him. In Pittsburgh, Andrew Carnegie and Richard Beattie Mellon – one in steel and the other in railroads – became distinguished clients. In New York, Henry Osborne Havemeyer (sugar refining) and Arthur Heckscher (minerals) followed suit, while the widows of railway magnates Jay Gould, Cornelius Vanderbilt and Russell Sage commissioned major memorials. Other memorials included those to ex-Presidents Benjamin Harrison (in the First Presbyterian Church in Indianapolis), Abraham Lincoln and Theodore Roosevelt (both in the Metropolitan Temple in New York City), and Chester A. Arthur (in the Trinity Church in Lenox, Mass.).

Certain windows have remained privileged. Those installed in the Wolf's Head secret society at Yale are for the sole appreciation of its members; the five commissioned by the Temple of the Latter Day Saints in Salt Lake City in the 1890s can be viewed only by Mormons. One of these, depicting Joseph Smith's "First Vision," is installed in the Temple's Holy of Holies, to which the head of the Church has exclusive access.

Tiffany's most important patron, however, was the picaresque sea captain-turned-capitalist, Joseph Raphael Delamar. Dutch-born, Delamar emigrated to America following numerous entrepreneurial ventures in the colonies. From 1878 he speculated in gold- and lead ore-mining in Colorado, Utah, and Idaho, accumulating a prodigious fortune in the conglomerates International Nickel, Dome, and

Nipissing. His remaining monument is the ghost town of Delamar in Idaho where he prospected for and found gold. Refusing the State's governorship, he settled in New York City where he bought a townhouse on Madison Avenue opposite J. P. Morgan's, and in 1911 he built a $15 million estate at Glen Cove on Long Island.

Delamar clearly loved Tiffany's windows, commissioning at least five, including "The Bathers" and a magnificent pair of bird panels for the Pompeian Room in his Madison Avenue home. His "Pembroke" estate at Glen Cove included a subterranean swimming pool illuminated by spherical Tiffany butterfly lampshades. Tiffany's international status brought respectability to the era's new money; it pursued him as eagerly as he did it.

The Ivy League was similarly well represented. Yale (the Chittenden Library), Dartmouth (Rollins Chapel), Princeton (the Alexander Commencement Hall), Harvard (Memorial Hall), Columbia (the Library), and Brown (St. Stephen's); other preeminent educational institutions were similarly embellished: Vassar, Smith, Wellesley, and Hotchkiss.

These windows were not inexpensive. The "Apocalypse" Simpson Memorial, installed in 1900 in the Calvary Methodist Church in Allegheny, cost $3,500 at a time when stained glass artisans were paid $3 per day and their supervisors $21 per week. The large "St. Paul Preaching to the Athenians" Memorial with its two flanking panels, in the Lafayette Avenue Presbyterian Church in Brooklyn, cost a colossal $5,000. For $700 the client could afford a medium-sized (5 ft. × 3 ft.) memorial. Tiffany lost more commissions because of high prices than for any other reason. An elderly communicant in the First Congregational Church in Toledo recalls vividly Tiffany's rage at being underpriced on one of the Church's commissions by the New York firm of Lederle & Geissler.

Window production at the Studios reached its high point between 1900 and 1910; thereafter output fell. The First World War, plus the public's increasing disinterest in Tiffany as a "new" phenomenon with each passing year, helped to accelerate this decline. As Tiffany himself aged – by 1920 he was seventy-two years old – his participation in, and control of, the firm diminished. The former exemplary standards slipped, if ever so slightly. Windows of the 1920s often have painted or roughly etched backgrounds, whereas previously only intricately leaded detailing would have sufficed. The time-consuming process of plating was likewise largely eliminated, resulting in brighter – even harsh – windows.

The decline in quality was matched by the public's loss of interest in stained glass as an art medium. Fashions had changed. By 1940 the new generation found Tiffany decidedly *passé*. His windows and – worse by far – those endlessly gaudy lamps dated one's home. The incriminating evidence was moved into attics and cellars or, more frequently, consigned to the trash heap.

The same fate awaited windows in institutions such as private clubs, hospitals, hotels, and theatres. Little effort was made to salvage them when the buildings in which they were installed surrendered to the bulldozer.

The major cause of attrition, however, has been the virtual demise of the church as a pillar of the urban community in the twentieth century. The Studios' earliest commissions coincided with a period of strong religious growth in America; its twilight years matched a pronounced downturn. The reason was in part ethnic and in part socio-economic. As industry and commerce lured workers to the inner city, overcrowding and unemployment resulted, leading in turn to increased crime and a decrease in the standard of living. The middle classes – the cornerstone of the neighborhood church and synagogue – fled to the suburbs. In most instances the church was given no choice but to uproot itself and follow its flock . . . or lose them. Where the churches stayed put, they were overhauled by the problem of how to keep operating as congregations declined, buildings aged, and maintenance costs rose. In the 1970s an average of twenty churches and synagogues were sold per year in New York City alone, often to make way for large apartment buildings. Sometimes churches with Tiffany windows have survived by merging or by selling to other, more buoyant, denominations. The predominantly white Christ Episcopal Church in New York's upper West Side became the Bible Deliverance Evangelistic Temple as the area's demographic balance shifted to black. Likewise, the South Third Street Presbyterian Church in Brooklyn became the Primera Iglesia Presbiteriana de Habla Española following the influx of Puerto Ricans into the neighborhood. Sometimes the Tiffany windows have survived the transition, in most cases they have not. For the majority of congregations the loss of its building has been the final symbol of dismemberment, the windows falling with it under the wrecker's ball.

The Chicago South Side surpasses even Manhattan and Boston in its dismal record of devastation. Between 1920 and 1970 all but one of twelve Tiffany churches fell: only the Second Presbyterian on Michigan Avenue has stood firm.

Fire has been far and away the greatest culprit. Its path of destruction has dogged Tiffany from the beginning. The conflagration which reduced one-half of Bangor, Maine, to ashes in 1911 took with it several churches; all that remains of the numerous splendid memorials in the First Presbyterian Church in Chillicothe, Ohio, is six square inches which survived a ruinous fire in 1956; the Chapel of the Association of the Home for the Relief of Respectable Aged and Indigent Females at 104th Street in Manhattan was the victim of an arsonist's whim during the city's 1977 blackout; faulty electrical wiring and dry rot combined to spark the blaze which melted the windows in the Congregational Church,

Montclair, New Jersey, in 1917 and the Marquand Chapel at Princeton in 1920. The number of fire casualties seems endless; the historian begins to suspect that he is facing a conspiracy.

Elsewhere, church windows have been torn from their frames and summarily smashed. Those in the First Universalist Church, Roxbury, Mass., all fell under the demolitionist's sledgehammer. In a few instances windows have been sold on being removed, as in the South Congregational Church in Peabody, Mass. The eight windows in the Church of the Unity, Cleveland, suffered a curious fate: four were sold and four stolen! All the mausoleums in the Mount Hope cemetery in Rochester, New York, have been stripped of their windows, while in the Cypress Lawn cemetery in San Francisco the researcher had been preceded by rock-throwing vandals. Vermont has the only recorded Tiffany window to be damaged by an ice fall.

Three generations later we must judge Tiffany's work anew. Fashions have changed again. Tiffany is back in favor and seems likely to remain so. Today one no longer quite raises one's eyebrows at the prospect of one of his major lamps selling for $250,000, an object made not of precious stones or gold but of glass and the alloy bronze – and not yet even an "antique" in the strict sense of the word. Clearly, Tiffany's work will finally be categorized as "Objects of Vertu," to be valued for workmanship and creativity rather than for intrinsic value. And if a lamp – an offshoot, after all, which evolved from the waste glass that accumulated from window-making – can be worth that much, what will the major windows themselves finally be worth? Till now their bulk and seeming immovability have held them back. Yet they represent Tiffany's highest aspiration, the driving force which dominated his creative energy for a full fifty years.

Critical analysis:
The critics on Tiffany

CONTEMPORARY CRITICS WERE in accord on the aesthetic merits of Tiffany's Favrile glass, which they felt heralded an enormously exciting new beginning. The infinite variations of color and richness promised beauty beyond measure. Far less enthusiastic, however, was their opinion on the designs of the windows within which this splendid material was to be placed. The German-French critic, Julius Meier-Graefe, went to the heart of the problem when he wrote in 1899 with great fervor, but also clear judgment, about Tiffany and his work. While noting that Tiffany's glass signified that the present had for once outdone the past, he was immediately careful to point out that he was referring to the color and the technique used, not the designs of the windows. He described the technique, its extraordinary complexity and consequent expense, and the method of plating to achieve modified tonal effects. Tiffany's marvelous technical skills enabled him to use mosaic as others used brushes on glass. The magnificent technique, however, served a design which was nowhere near the same level. In the creation of windows, Tiffany's talents lay almost entirely in the realm of color. On the other hand, Tiffany's vases were above reproach and beyond compare. Meier-Graefe found them so original, so admirable, so aesthetically complete, that he even expressed doubts that the vases and windows stemmed from the same hand.

The English critic, Horace Townsend, had similar misgivings when he viewed the 1899 Grafton Gallery exhibition in London. He singled out for particular mention and praise windows "where figure subjects or indeed patterns themselves are altogether abandoned, and the whole effect is derived from the display of glass itself in all its glories or gorgeously blended colors."

Much later, Herwin Schaefer wrote, in discussing such turn-of-the-century censure, that "even now, at the height of his fame, the beauty and richness of the glass did not blind the critics to the frequent inadequacy of Tiffany's designs, an inadequacy which was basically one of misusing his decorative material for pictorial purposes. When he created a window

"King David the Psalmist," Memorial diptych; original Tiffany Studios photograph of unrecorded window.

entitled 'The Flight of the Soul' which is described as having a figure of Christ in the centre with figures of souls veering towards him, one understands the critic who called it 'froid, triste, obscur' even though it was made of Tiffany's justly famous glass. However, the lower part of this window was taken up by bushes of flowers which actually served merely as a pretext to introduce elements of color, and this part of the window shows Tiffany to much better advantage because he does not try to serve ideas or sentiment but lets the magic of his material speak in its own right."

In certain instances one must agree. Many of Tiffany's religious windows, in particular, portrayed a maudlin, overweening nineteenth-century sentimentality at a time when the artists and writers of the period, such as Paul Gauguin and the French poet Stéphane Mallarmé, insisted that the work of art must *suggest* experiences and sensibilities rather than simply state them.

Tiffany found himself caught between two constituencies: on the one hand, the demands of his conservative clients, and on the other, those of the art world. The customers who commissioned religious figure windows to adorn their churches in memory of a deceased relative sought a traditional interpretation of a Biblical theme. They were unaware of, and would certainly have been uninfluenced by, what the critics at the international expositions determined as fashionable. They knew what they liked and what they liked was traditional. Tiffany soon learned that he would have to keep the two apart if he was to retain their respective loyalties. A special set of windows were therefore designed for exhibition purposes. These were floral, abstract, and ornamental in theme. Gone were the St. Michael and St. Joseph of earlier expositions; in their place rich, glowing hydrangeas and poppies in heavily layered and "fractured" glass. The effect was romantic and impressionistic. The critics were appeased.

The designers

TIFFANY DESIGNED MOST, if not all, of the firm's early windows. Important commissions in the 1880s, such as the one for Miss Elizabeth Garrett of Baltimore, were from his own hand, often a direct translation of one of his earlier watercolors or oils. Administrative duties increasingly ate into his time, however, and qualified designers had to be brought into the firm to meet the increasing demand for windows which Tiffany generated in his role as entrepreneur.

By 1890 the nucleus of the Design Department which would serve him so faithfully for the next several decades had been formed. Tiffany continued to design the most prestigious commissions – those for a Mellon, Delamar, or Havemeyer – as well as Exposition windows such as "The Four Seasons" and those for the 1893 Chicago World's Fair. With each year, however, his contribution decreased, although from the start he maintained ultimate control of *all* designs. Nothing was shown to the client without his approval. Cartoons which do not bear Tiffany's full signature have his initials under the heading *Approved by*. Frequently one sees corrections pencilled into the margin of preliminary sketches, such as "scale too small" or "delete one figure."

Tiffany drew on whatever inspiration was necessary to meet the customer's needs. When his own designs were inappropriate, others would serve as well. A number of windows, for example, were taken from paintings by Old Masters. Carracci's "The Holy Family," Raphael's "Transfiguration," Ingres' "The Apotheosis of Homer," Murillo's "The Annunciation," and Gustave Doré's later "Christ Leaving the Praetorium" were reproduced, often with slight variations, more than once.

The cartoon for a transept window by Frederick Wilson, 1905, entitled "He took her by the hand and the maid arose;" watercolor on board with superimposed cardboard mullions and tracery.

Tiffany drew frequently also on nineteenth-century painters. The German Heinrich Hoffman was a favorite. The Church of the Unity in Springfield, Mass., had two windows executed from his paintings; another is to be found in the Lafayette Avenue Presbyterian Church, Brooklyn; and almost all the

·SKETCH·N4·

·SCHEME·A·

IN
·SACRED·MANY·YEARS·
ABCDFG·DE·HLIKE·
1876···1932·
·FOR·MANY·YEARS·
·ORGANIST·AND·CHOIR·
·MASTER·AT·THIS·CHURCH·

·SCHEME·B·

·SCALE· ½"=1'·0"·

·SUGGESTION·FOR·
·GLASS·MOSAIC·TABLET·
·WITH·WOOD·FRAME·

The cartoon for a Memorial to H.T. Smith, Chicago; watercolor on board. (Collection of the Albany Institute of History and Art.)

◁ A sketch from the Ecclesiastical Department for a church aisle, showing, from the left, a window, mosaic Memorial tablet, and carved wooden door beneath three lancet windows.

◁ A typical completed sketch from the Ecclesiastical Department ready to be shown to the client following Tiffany's approval. The scale is shown on the right.

"The Three Magi," a cartoon for a Memorial lancet window. ▷

windows in the Middle Dutch Church in Manhattan are direct translations of his works. Holman Hunt's "Christ Knocking at the Door" was another painting executed in glass.

Tiffany clearly did not wish to borrow too frequently from other sources in this manner. He was, however, a pragmatic businessman who realized only too well that if a customer wished to have a favorite painting reproduced as a memorial he could take the commission elsewhere if Tiffany refused.

Considering the enormous volume of windows which were produced, there are remarkably few duplicates. Whereas the First Presbyterian Church in Lockport, New York, and the First Congregational Church in Augusta, Maine, for example, have windows of King David in which the central figure is identical, the dimensions and the backgrounds of the two are different. Likewise, the "Four Elements" windows in the Second Reformed Church, Hackensack, and the Shepard Memorial Church in Boston employ an identical central theme on different backgrounds. The Studio was proud of its claim that each window commission was unique; in the one or two instances where it bent this dictum, it covered its trail by placing these windows in churches of different denominations thousands of miles apart.

The cartoon for the grape arbor window in *La Belle Verrière* restaurant, Winter Park, Florida, owned by Mr. and Mrs. McKean. The cartoon is in the Avery Library at Columbia University.

28 "The Bathers," one of Tiffany's most important windows. Installed in Laurelton Hall (see p. 161), it was destroyed when the mansion was gutted by fire in 1957. The window may not, as has generally been believed, have been designed by Tiffany for his own home. The list of illustrations in C. Dekay, *The Art Work of Louis C. Tiffany*, New York 1914, describes the window as "designed for Captain J. R. Delamar in 1912." Perhaps Tiffany decided to keep it or Delamar did not want the completed commission. (*Photo: courtesy of Howard Ellman*)

29 A figure window depicting an unidentified woman and her daughter. The shadows on the ground are achieved by layering on the back of the window.

30 A charming figure window depicting an unidentified young woman amongst foliage.

31 This window is installed on a stairway landing in one of the buildings in the Wayne Community College, Detroit, Michigan. It is flanked by five smaller panels depicting musical instruments.

32 This portrait window is an exact copy of Jules Lefebvre's *La Liseuse* (The Reader), which was displayed at the Paris Salon in 1889. (*Photo: courtesy of Dr. Egon Neustadt*)

33 This landscape window was commissioned by Webb Horton for the stairway in the forty-room mansion which he built in Middletown, New York, in 1902. In 1950 the estate became the home of the Orange County Community College.

In Affectionate Memory of his Father and Mother By Waldr W Law ✝✝✝✝✝✝✝

JOHN·BOYD 1799-1881   EMILY·W·BOYD 1805-1842

(*Facing page*)

34 This landscape window was donated to the Congregational Church, Briarcliff Manor, New York, by Walter W. Law in memory of his parents, *c.* 1898.

35 The John and Emily Boyd landscape Memorial in the Second Congregational Church (now the Church of Christ, Baptist, Congregational), Winsted, Connecticut, 1898.

36 "The Stream of Life," the Memorial to Sydenham C. Parsons and Harriet Electa Parsons in the Congregational Church, Northampton, Mass., which was unveiled by one of their children, Mrs. Arthur Curtis James, in 1899. The Studios considered it an exceptional example of a landscape window, and illustrated it in two of their booklets.

37 The landscape window commissioned by Howard Hinds for the sandstone mansion which he built in Euclid Heights, Cleveland, *c.* 1900. Tiffany decorated the entire house, providing green striped satin walls, rich moiré and satin draperies, and gilded Louis XVI furnishings in a manner similar to that in which he had decorated the White House twenty years earlier. The window was subsequently donated to the Cleveland Museum of Art by Mrs. Robert M. Fallon, Mr. Hinds' daughter.

38 The Margaret Standart Watson Memorial in the Central Presbyterian Church (now the Westminster Presbyterian), Auburn, New York, given by Mrs. Watson's daughter, Janet Seward, *c.* 1900.

39   "St. John's Vision of the Holy City," the Charles
B. Knight Memorial in St. John's Episcopal Church,
Troy, New York, *c.* 1900.

40 "At Evening Time It Shall Be Light," the James R. Taylor Memorial window in the First Presbyterian Church, Brooklyn, 1901.

41 This landscape window was commissioned by Charles Rushmore for his mansion, "Carmore," at Woodbury Falls, New York, c. 1900. It was installed at the head of the stairway landing.

◁ 42 The Johnson Memorial window in the First Congregational Church of Minnesota, Minneapolis. Removed during construction many years ago, it was recently discovered in a coal bin in the basement and re-installed.

43 The Jonathan French Memorial in St. Paul's Episcopal Church, Nantucket, Mass. The Church, erected by Caroline French in memory of her father, Jonathan, has several other floral windows.

44   "Holy City," the John Webster Oothout Memorial in the Third Presbyterian Church, Rochester, New York, *c.* 1902. Jerusalem is shown through the clouds.

◁ 45   "New Jerusalem," the Judson Memorial installed in 1903 in the May Memorial Unitarian Church, Syracuse, New York. It interprets the Biblical text: "And I John saw the holy city, new Jerusalem coming down from God." The window is now in the Everson Museum of Art, Syracuse.

46   "Benedicite," the Michael Miller Memorial in the Trinity Episcopal Church, Staunton, Virginia, *c.* 1902. The Millers were an old parish family.

47   A detail of the window designed by Agnes   ▷ Northrop as a Memorial to her father, Allen Parkhill Northrop, in the Reformed Church, Flushing, Long Island, 1903.

◁ 48 "Peace," the Ann Eliza Brainerd Smith landscape Memorial in the First Congregational Church, St. Albans, Vermont, *c.* 1905.

49 "The Water Brooks Window," the Memorial to Ezekiel Hayes Trowbridge installed in the First Church of Christ in New Haven, Conn., 1904. When the church was restored in 1960, the window was one of three donated to the Southern Connecticut State College, where it was installed in the campus library.

50 The Emma and John Pennington Memorial in the Bay Head Chapel, Bay Head, New Jersey, *c.* 1904, possibly depicting the nearby Barnicut lighthouse.

51 The landscape window in the First Presbyterian Church, ▷ Far Rockaway, Long Island, commissioned by Mrs. Russell Sage in memory of her husband, *c.* 1905. One of Tiffany's finest and largest windows, it was illustrated in the 1913 booklet, *Memorials in Glass and Stone.*

52　The Greysolon Dulhut Memorial commissioned by the Daughters of the American Revolution for the Dulhut Public Library and formally presented on November 9th, 1904, at a cost of $750. Designed by a local artist, Mrs. Anne Weston, in honor of the French explorer after whom the city is named, the window depicts the bluffs where the city now stands as he would have seen them from the Wisconsin shore of Lake Superior. The upper frieze includes the inscription "Quo sursum volo videre" ("I wish to see what is beyond"), which was the original motto on the Territory's seal, and a band of moccasin flowers, the Minnesota emblem. The lower section shows a French *fleur-de-lis* and flintlock of the *coureur des bois*.

53　Melchior S. Belthoover, an oil and cotton baron from Natchez, Mississippi, commissioned this landscape window for the 44-room stone castle "Rochroanne" which he built at Irvington-on-Hudson between 1902 and 1904. The price was $3,200. The window, which was illustrated in *The International Studio*, XXVI, 1905, xvii, p. XV, is now in the Corning Museum of Glass. Anemones and hollyhock bloom beneath pendant trumpet vines and clematis.

54 A domestic landscape window commissioned for a solarium in a Newark, New Jersey, house, *c.* 1905. Two vases of cabbage roses flank a marble fountain carved with a satyr whose mouth houses a water pipe.

55 A triptych domestic window depicting red hollyhocks in a landscape.

56   The Frederic Henry Betts Memorial window in St. Andrew's Dune Church, Southampton, Long Island, *c.* 1906. Betts was a founder and trustee of the church.

57   "The Earth is the Lord's and the fullness thereof," the William Goddard Memorial in St. Luke's Episcopal Church, East Greenwich, Rhode Island. *c.* 1908.

58   The Snowden Memorial window in the Bryn
Mawr Presbyterian Church, Pa., c. 1910. (*Photo:
G. Smith*)

59   The Frederick A. Wilcoxson landscape Memorial
in St. John's Episcopal Church, North Adams, Mass.,
1910, depicting a garden in the Holy Land.

60 The landscape window commissioned by Richard B. Mellon for the stairway landing of his house at 6500 Fifth Avenue, Pittsburgh, 1908–1912. Six of the ten panels (shown in black and white) were destroyed when the house was torn down in 1940. The surviving four (illustrated in colour) are in the Carnegie Institute.

Tiffany's most prominent designers stayed with the firm for many years. Others, such as Henry Keck, stayed only a while before branching out on their own. Keck established a studio near Syracuse, New York, and decorated numerous houses in the vicinity with his Tiffanyesque windows and panels. Others, again, like the artisans in the Window and Lamp Departments, moved from firm to firm as the workload demanded. If Tiffany's was quiet, his nearby competitor, Lamb Studios, might have taken on a new commission which required extra help at that moment. Their skills were common to all stained glass firms and were thus interchangeable. This is the reason, incidentally, why the style of painting on windows from two different studios often bears an uncanny similarity; the same artist may well have painted both.

The principal designer after Tiffany himself was Frederick Wilson. For over thirty years his output and versatility were phenomenal. Several of his window designs were included in the 1893 Chicago Exposition and as late as 1923 he designed the "Te Deum Laudamus" mosaic triptych in the First Methodist Church, Los Angeles. Wilson designed all types of religious and secular windows and mosaic friezes. His predilection, however, was for figure windows. The 1897 Tiffany Studios booklet *Memorial Windows*, for example, illustrated a wide range of his designs for windows, such as "The Ascension," "The Archangel Raphael," "The Lord is my Shepherd," "Easter Morning," and perhaps his most popular theme, "Christ Blessing Little Children." He also designed "The Last Supper" mosaic in the First Independent Christ Church, Baltimore. The Appendix to the 1897 List of Windows contains numerous letters from customers paying tribute to Wilson's designs.

Edward Peck Sperry, from New Haven, Conn., was another member of the Design Department who joined the firm around 1890. He was credited with several windows in

A Tiffany Studios photograph of the cartoon for the Chittenden window at Yale. The upper panel was apparently never completed as it was not installed with the lower section. (See color plate 26.)

"The Good Samaritan," a cartoon for a Memorial window in one of the Ecclesiastical Department's booklets, *Tributes to Honor*. The Biblical story has been adapted to the Civil War.

The cartoon for the Asbury
Memorial in the First Methodist
Church, Los Angeles; watercolor on board. (Collection of
the Albany Institute of History
and Art)

The Design Room at Tiffany
Studios, *c.* 1913.

(*Facing page*) The Glass Shop
at the Studios, *c.* 1913, showing a
large number of glaziers
selecting glass and assembling
windows.

The Mosaic Shop at Tiffany
Studios, *c.* 1914. Mosaicists can
be seen working on altar crosses
and architectural friezes.

the Chicago Exposition, plus "St. Andrew," "The
Resurrection," and "The Nativity" in *Memorial Windows*. A
major project was his "Ivanhoe" window for the University
of Chicago in 1904. There is a series of Dutch eighteenth-
century style panels in the Congregational Church, Plymouth,
Mass., painted by Sperry in 1910 in heavy sepia enamels,
suggesting that by then he had left the Studies.

Joseph Lauber headed his own studio before joining Tiffany
in the early 1890s. He designed a wide range of windows,
such as "The Angel of Praise" illustrated in the 1897 booklet
and "John Davenport preaching to the Colonists of New
Haven" in the Centre Church, New Haven. Lauber also
designed liturgical items such as altars, sedilia, and predellae.
One mosaic frieze in a Studios booklet is attributed to both
Lauber and Edwin Blashfield.

J. A. Holzer was another who was lured from self-
employment to join the firm. He, too, was a most
accomplished artist, designing everything from the colossal
sanctuary lamp in the Church of the Covenant, Boston, to
windows such as "The Vision of St. John." His major works,

however, were in mosaics: the 120 ft.-long frieze depicting the exploration of the Northwest Passage by Marquette and Joliet in 1673 in the Marquette Building, Chicago; the Heros and Heroines of the Homeric story in the Alexander Commencement Hall at Princeton; and the incredibly fine mosaic dome and frescoes (containing literally millions of glass sectiliae and tesserae) in the Chicago Public Library to the designs of the architects Shipley, Rutan, & Coolidge. Examples of Holzer's windows prior to his joining Tiffany can be seen in St. Paul's Episcopal Church, Troy, New York, and the Convent Chapel at Elmhurst, Providence. Holzer was succeeded by Joseph Briggs when he retired.

Selecting sheets of glass from the racks at the Corona Studios. Notice the wooden lamp molds.

The Shade Shop at the Studios. Several lamp models are recognizable. John Dikeman, who later headed the department, is seen standing second from the right.

A rare view of a glazier at the Studios weatherproofing a finished window by the light of an Edison bulb. The photograph was found at Laurelton Hall in the 1950s.

A signed watercolor sketch on paper mounted on canvas by Agnes Northrop.

A signed watercolor sketch on paper mounted on canvas by Agnes Northrop of flowering magnolia blossoms.

"Behold the Western Evening Light," the cartoon for the Coburn Memorial designed by Agnes Northrop for the Eliot Congregational Church, Newton, Mass. The window was destroyed when the church was gutted by fire in the 1950s.

A sketch by Agnes Northrop for a Memorial landscape window.

One of the few women members of the design department (another was Clara Driscoll, nee Wolcott, who designed the popular dragonfly lampshade), Agnes Northrop joined Tiffany in 1884 at the age of 27. Initially in the women's glass department under Miss Anne Vanderlip, she later moved to the design department where she designed floral and landscape windows for forty years. Among the numerous notable commissions which she undertook were those for Miss Helen Gould and Andrew Carnegie (see pp. 166 and 170). Her work, which included memorials to her mother and father, can be seen in the Reformed Church, Flushing, Long Island. Miss Northrop outlasted all her colleagues, joining Charles Nussbaum, John Berrian, and Edward Stanton when they formed the Westminster Memorial Studios on 23rd and 26th

Agnes Northrop's watercolor sketch for the triptych landscape window commissioned by Mr. H. Mariss for the stairway landing of his house in Shanghai, China. The panels depict hollyhocks, foxgloves, peonies, and larkspur.

Streets in New York City in 1933 to complete Tiffany's outstanding commissions. Miss Northrop retired in 1936 and died in the early 1950s at the age of 96.

The last of the important designers was Will H. Low. Already an accomplished designer when he joined the firm – his article "Old Glass in New Windows" was published in *Scribner's Magazine* in 1888 – he appears to have started in the early 1890s, as a memorial of his was included in the 1893 Chicago Exposition. Other windows included the Chapin Memorial and "Gloria in Excelsis" in the Church of the Unity, Springfield, Mass. Another fine example is the "Blessed are the Pure in Heart" Bartol Memorial in the First Unitarian Church, Philadelphia.

Other designers whose names appear in the Studios' booklets were Lydia Emmet, John Berrian, René de Quelin, Howard Pyle, and Lydia Carr, who designed the "Christ and the Four Evangelists" Howland Memorial in the Church of the Heavenly Rest, New York.

The window department

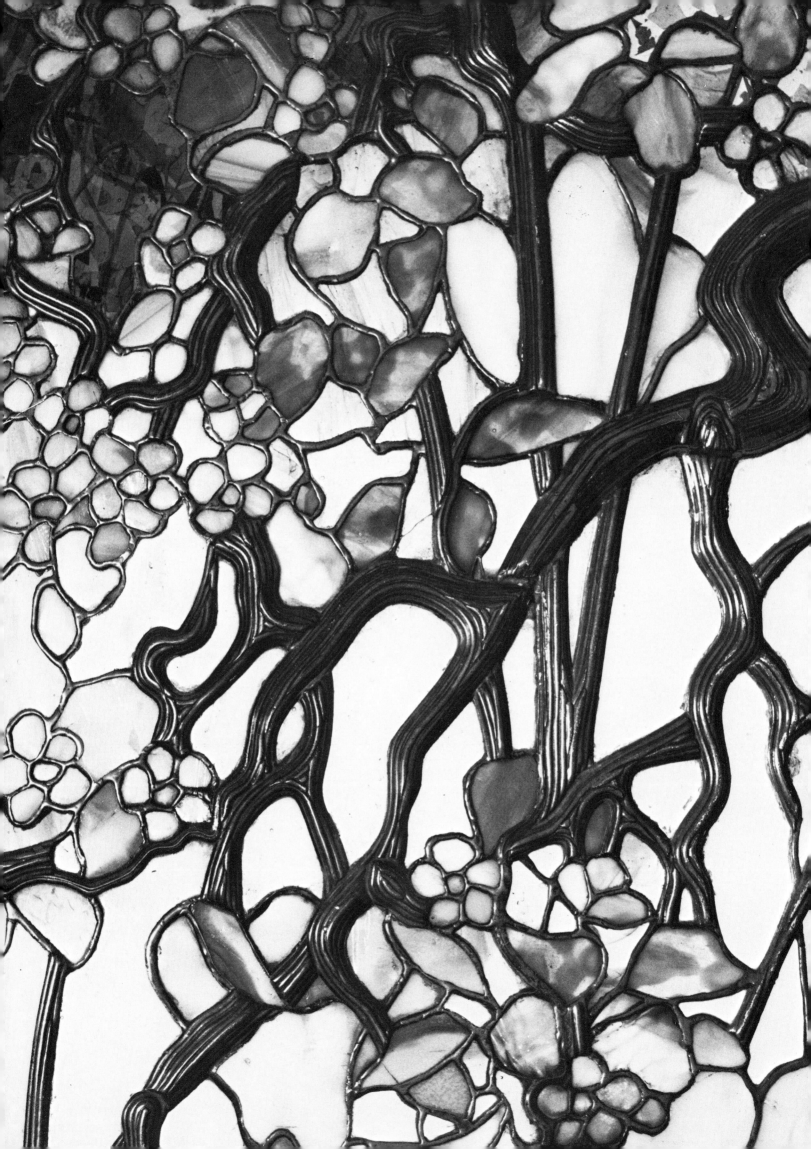

N O INFORMATION HAS SURVIVED on the numbers of artisans employed in the Window Department of Tiffany's through the years. The Lamp Shop, its offshoot, grew to nearly 200 strong. It is unlikely that that many were ever employed directly in window production, but if one adds those involved both directly and indirectly at both ends of the operation – on the one end, the designers, and on the other, the team of technicians who crated, and travelled with, the windows to install them – the total must have been considerable.

A most unusual characteristic of the Studios was the high proportion of young women who worked as artisans in this traditionally male profession. The circumstances which precipitated this were described by Cecilia Waern in *International Studio* in 1897: "When Mr. Tiffany first started his workshops, he soon found out, as the starter of Merton Abbey had done, that the only way to get his ideas carried out was by training boys to the work from the beginning. So he employed such workmen as were to be had, putting boys under them as apprentices. After a while the men struck on the score of too many apprentices. Mr. Tiffany let them all go, replaced them by young women from the art schools where they had at least learned to use their eyes and their fingers in certain ways, and trained them himself. At present there are from forty to fifty young women employed in the glass workshop, working at either mosaic or windows, generally ornamental." Other female duties involved wrapping the cut pieces of glass in copper foil for lamps and panels.

Tiffany frequently praised the women's manual dexterity, color sensitivity, and proficiency in cutting glass. It is probably not unfair to note that while he had one eye on their skills, the other was on the low wages which they earned; 60 per cent of that of their male counterparts.

The technique which the Studios employed in assembling its windows was the same as that used by its competitors. Briefly, the process – basically the same today as it was

A detail of an apple blossom window showing how the lead came has been realistically milled to simulate the texture of the bark on the branches. Tiffany applied the same attention to detail on some of his more important lampshades, especially the "spider web" model. (*Photo courtesy of the Virginia Museum of Art, Richmond*)

described in the twelfth century by the monk Theophilus in his *Book of Various Arts* – is as follows: the size and shape of the window having been chosen, the artist-designer prepares a color sketch to show the customer. On approval, a full-size cartoon is produced, from which two paper transfers are made. One of these is kept as a later guide for the glazier. The other is divided up with a special double-bladed knife which removes a 1/16th-in. strip between each piece to allow for the lead calmes. The pieces of paper, known as paper patterns or templates, are positioned on a large clear glass easel on which the lead lines are drawn in black. The easel is then set against a light source. The cutter, under the supervision of the artist, next chooses a sheet of glass for a section of the window, removing the paper pattern from the easel so that he can hold the sheet to the light. When satisfied that he has found the piece of glass which best meets his color needs, he marks the area on the sheet which is to be used. The paper pattern is then placed on this spot and scored along its edges with a diamond cutter. The piece of glass is separated from the sheet and grozed to remove any rough edges. When it corresponds *exactly* to the paper pattern, it is attached to the easel with a small blob of wax. The window is assembled in this way like a giant multi-colored jigsaw puzzle, each piece of glass replacing its paper pattern until the entire window is cut and placed on the easel. The artist checks the window's progress continually, modifying the original color scheme as he thinks fit. At times plating is used to obtain a particular shade or tint. When all the pieces have been assembled, those which are to be painted are sent to the artist and replaced on their return. The window then passes to the glazier to be leaded.

It can be seen from the above that Tiffany demanded enormous abilities and attention from an artist-designer. He or she had to superintend each stage of production to ensure that the translation from sketch to window incorporated every optimum color combination and nuance that the glass could

These three illustrations trace the main stages in the production of a Tiffany window. Shown is "The Education of the Virgin," the Marie Louisa Vanderbilt Memorial designed by Frederick Wilson for the Grace Episcopal Church in Madison, New Jersey, in 1897: the cartoon, the glass easel with some of the paper patterns attached, and the finished window.

afford. Sometimes he would even oversee the making of the glass itself. Not the least of Tiffany's contributions to the art of stained glass was his ability to train artist-artisans to utilize his inventions in glass to maximum effect. His own enthusiasm and creativity proved infectious, as did his daily reminder that "infinite endless labor makes the masterpiece."

GLASS

It was Tiffany's inimitable glass which set him apart from all competitors and predecessors. Sometimes as many as seven different ladles were thrown together on to the table and then rolled by hand or machine into irregular sheets which, when annealed, would be carefully labelled by color and texture. Cecilia Waern wrote, following a visit to the Corona factory in 1897, that the stock of 200 to 300 *tons* of glass in the cellar comprised over 5,000 different colors and varieties of glass stored and catalogued in cases, compartments, and shelves, all labelled or numbered as neatly as office records in a filing cabinet, and as easily accessible. The artist had an unlimited palette at his fingertips.

Below are described some of the techniques – those identifiable elements within each window – which have become the hallmarks of Tiffany's mastery of the medium.

Mottled glass: This most characteristic and immediately identifiable of Tiffany's numerous varieties was the most difficult to create. It required the most rigid temperature controls. Basically, the chemical fluorine was incorporated into a heavily viscous, lead-based glass. Fluorine is a crystalline substance which begins to collect in the glass (glass is a fluid, *not* a solid) during annealing in different patterns at different temperatures. The technique was implemented in every color, sometimes in deeply pulsating two-color combinations.

61　This pair of windows represents the highpoint of Tiffany's domestic stained glass production. Commissioned by Captain Joseph R. Delamar for the Pompeian Room in his town house at Madison Avenue and 37th Street, New York, *c.* 1912, they were later transferred to Delamar's country estate "Pembroke" at Glen Cove, Long Island. The left-hand panel depicts a cockatoo eating cherries beneath two parakeets; the companion panel shows a peacock on a balustrade beneath pendant wisteria. The two were illustrated in *Memorials in Glass and Stone*, 1913; *Arts and Decoration*, June 1913, p. 288; and discussed in *The New York Herald Magazine*, December 26th, 1915, p. 12.

IN MEMORY OF REDFIELD PROCTOR ✠ 1831 - 1908
✠ FOUNDER OF THIS VILLAGE AND ITS INDUSTRY ✠

THE STRENGTH OF THE HILLS IS HIS ALSO ✠ Psalm xcv 4

IN memory of FLETCHER DUTTON PROCTOR 1860-1911
HE WROUGHT CHRISTIAN BROTHERHOOD INTO THE COMMUNITY ✠

ALL ISRAEL AND JUDAH LOVED DAVID FOR HE WENT
OUT AND CAME IN BEFORE THEM ✠ I SAM XVIII 16

◁ 62　The Redfield Proctor diptych in the
Union Church, Proctor, Vermont,
depicting a vista along a wooded river
towards Pico Peak, near Rutland. The
window was installed *c.* 1909 by the
Proctor family as a Memorial to the
founder of the Proctor marble company
from whom the town took its name.

◁ 63　The Fletcher Dutton Proctor
Memorial in the Union Church,
Proctor, Vermont. Installed *c.* 1912, the
diptych depicts a view of the Proctor
valley from the southwest towards Lake
Champlain. The church's spire is visible
in the central panel of the left-hand
window.

64　The Sarah Fay Sumner Memorial
installed in the Sunday School room at
the First Reformed Church, Albany,
New York, 1912. Mrs. Sumner was an
active member of the congregation who
taught Sunday School for 44 years.
Some years ago the window was slightly
damaged during a basketball game and
moved to its present location behind a
stairway.

65   The Alice McElroy landscape
Memorial in the First Presbyterian
Church, Albany, New York, *c.* 1914.

UNTIL·THE·DAY·BREAK·
AND·THE·SHADOWS·FLEE·AWAY·   TO·THE·GLORY·OF·GOD·AND·IN·LOVING·MEMOR
ALICE·McELROY·   DIED·MARCH·1·1913·AT·BARDEZAG
WIFE·OF·JOHN·HOWARD·KINGSBURY·

66 The William Neil Strong and Sarah Adelaide Knox Strong Memorial in the First Presbyterian Church, Albany, New York, presented by their daughter, Sarah, in 1915. The five panels are surmounted by three large medallion rose windows.

67 The Memorial window in the Second Presbyterian Church, Chicago, commissioned in 1918 by Mrs. C. D. Ettinger to commemorate her husband's love of the outdoors. The church, which was rebuilt by the architects Shaw and Bartlett after a fire in 1900, contains a wide range of fine windows by Tiffany, La Farge, Burne-Jones, Healy and Millet, and McCully and Miles.

68　This magnificent landscape window was presented by Mrs. Mary L. Hartwell to the Central Baptist Church, Providence, Rhode Island, as a Memorial to her husband, Frederick W. Hartwell. Installed in the chancel in April 1917, it took eight months to complete, becoming the largest landscape commission ever undertaken by the studios. The theme is based on Psalm 121: 1, 2: "I will lift up mine eyes unto the hills, from whence cometh my help. My help cometh from the Lord, which made heaven and earth." Fierce controversy erupted within the congregation when it was learned that the intended window did not depict any religious figures, such as Christ or Adoring Angels.

69   This landscape window was taken from a Mr. Hill's residence in Tarrytown, New York. Dated 1920, the window incorporates several of Tiffany's favorite themes: a peacock, sailing ships, balustrade, and pendant wisteria clusters.

70   "Whence Cometh my Help," the Foot Memorial in the Church of the Unity, Springfield, Mass. A booklet published by the church in 1929 states that the window was designed by Russell Foot, a boy in the congregation, in memory of his grandparents. The window was removed when the church was torn down in the 1960s. It is now in a private collection.

71　A fine landscape memorial window, *c.* 1920.

72 The Charles Duncan and William G. Hegardt Memorial in the Pilgrim Congregational Church, Duluth, Minnesota, *c.* 1924. Daffodils and irises bloom beneath pendant wisteria.

73 A landscape window in memory of Louise Holbrook Bett in St. Andrew's Dune Church, Southampton, Long Island.

74 "River of Life," the Willis L. Ogden Memorial in the First Presbyterian Church, Brooklyn, 1921.

Charles A Duncan
December 25th 1858 — July 13th 1924

William G Hegardt
March 27th 1860 — September 22nd

75   A triptych Memorial window
depicting a fawn drinking at a stream.
The inscription gives the scene a
religious connotation, *c.* 1922.

"AS·THE·HART·PANTETH·AFTER
THE·WATER·BROOKS·SO·PANTETH
MY·SOUL·AFTER·THEE· O·GOD"

76 The Abbie Goodale Hoopes Memorial in the Pilgrim Congregational Church, Duluth, Minnesota. The window was dedicated in honor of the Church's fiftieth anniversary in 1921.

77 The Minnie E. Proctor Memorial in the Union Church, Proctor, Vermont, depicting a view of Mount Mansfield in northern Vermont, where Mrs. Proctor was born. The window was installed in 1928.

IN·MEMORY·OF
1865 MINNIE·E·PROCTOR 1928

THROUGH·LOVE·TO·LIGHT·OH·WONDERFVL·THE·WAY

78 "River of Life," a landscape Memorial window depicting red poppies, cypress trees and flowering magnolias in a riverscape (private collection).

79 The Bigelow Memorial window (private collection).

80 "Rest," one of five panels depicting the four seasons (the fifth panel is entitled "all the seasons") in the Battell Chapel, Church of Christ Congregational, Norfolk, Connecticut. Donated by Mrs. Carl Stoeckel, the panel represents Winter, taking its theme from Psalm 127, v. 2: "He giveth his beloved sleep."

81 This superb triptych window is installed in St. James Country Club, outside Perryopolis, Pa. The central fountain is flanked by a profusion of summer flowers. Each panel is 80 in. wide.

82 The Frank Memorial window depicting irises beneath flowering magnolia in a landscape (private collection).

83 A beautiful landscape window depicting flowering bushes to the front of a distant mountain range (private collection).

Drapery glass: Unlike other glass techniques which Tiffany saw in their experimental stages and was quick to preempt and develop to the point where they became his own, drapery glass really was his own invention. Created to simulate the folds in the vestments worn by the Biblical figures in his religious windows, drapery glass was a natural corollary of his rejection of painted glass. It proved also to be his greatest challenge, the prize which eluded him longer than any other.

The glass, while still molten, was thrown onto an iron table and rolled into a disk. The glassmaker, clad in thick asbestos gloves and armed with tongs, then manipulated the glass mass, as one would pastry dough, by taking hold of it from both ends and pulling and twisting till it fell into folds. Where necessary, pliers were used to help form the corrugations. All colors of drapery were made in various degrees of translucency. The gradation of color was so realistic that drapery glass was soon used in a multitude of different ways, especially for the petals in magnolia and Easter lily floral panels and lampshades.

Fractured glass: Known today also as "confetti" glass, this was a revival and modification of the old Venetian method of embedding bits of colored glass into sheets of clear glass. Irregular colored chips and fragments of glass were scattered onto an iron table, on which the gaffer then poured the hot gather of glass. This was rolled flat in the usual manner, pressing the offcuts into the underside of the glass. "Fractured" glass proved highly effective for backgrounds in landscape and floral windows, providing a diffused impression of looking through variegated foliage.

Glass jewels: The Corona glassworks produced an inexhaustible range of glass jewels in every color, size, and shape. The molten glass was pressed into molds to form ovals or faceted prisms which, when set into the window, would produce brilliant gem-like effects, changing their shades of color and brilliance as the viewer changed his position. Jewels are ubiquitous in Tiffany's windows – as encrusted crowns, crucifixes, flower centers, and, most frequently, as accents in geometric borders. A large variation was the "turtle-back tile," its surface afterwards heightened with rainbow iridescence.

Etched glass: "Flashed" glass consists of two or more colored layers rolled together while still molten to form a single sheet. The application of hydrochloric acid and an acid-resistant wax to the surface of the glass eats away (etches) the exposed areas to create two- or multi-colored designs.

Tiffany employed the technique selectively as an improvement on the time-honored method of applying stain and enamel to glass to provide detail (both are opaque and therefore block the passage of light through the window). A highly realistic effect was achieved, for example, by etching a flashed opaque white-on-orange glass to produce the horizontal cloud formations in the sunsets so prevalent in Tiffany landscape windows.

Plating: This technique originated in America through the efforts of stained glass artists to improve on the lifeless, monochromatic European glass which they were forced to purchase from New York glass importers. The exasperated artist placed one or more pieces of glass on top of the initial layer to try to introduce greater depth of color and increased vibrancy. La Farge traced the technique's origin to the 1876 Philadelphia Centennial Exposition, explaining that "a figure window was made in this manner, that is, of glass not painted on, but very much according to the laws of complementary colors . . . certain European artists and commissioners of the Exposition happening to notice this (unfortunate) piece of

A detail of the back of a Tiffany window showing how a second layer of glass has been plated on to the back of the window in places to create certain light effects which the original piece of glass did not provide on its own.

work not only recognized a new departure, but expressed the hope of some future possibilities."

Tiffany took these possibilities further than anyone else. By employing two or more layers (there is at least one extant window which incorporates six layers), he was able to create densities and richness impossible within a single sheet. As he himself explained in 1893, "colored glass as an artistic medium has been at all times a most difficult material to work with, as in the main it is unyielding and fixed in form and color, when once it has left the furnace. The American artist, to overcome this, has resorted to plating one piece of glass over another, so that when in one sheet of glass we may find form and movement which is demanded by the sketch and cartoon but which has not the color sought, we secure the color by plating over or under the glass another glass of a different color or of another tone of the same color, which in combination give the effect desired."

Tiffany plated on both the front and back of his windows; the former tending to diffuse and soften the light, the latter providing perspective to landscapes.

The leading: Not content to limit his innovations to the glass in his windows, Tiffany revolutionized the design concept of the leading which held the pieces of glass together.

Traditionally, lead lines provided support, not design. If they crisscrossed the window haphazardly – bisecting an arm or robe en route – this was necessary to ensure that all parts were adequately reinforced. On eliminating paint from his windows, Tiffany had to rely on the leading to provide the lost detail whether, in so doing, it supported the glass *or not*.

New dies were ordered to provide a wide range of lead widths from $1/8$ in. to $1\frac{1}{2}$ in. These, when interspersed judiciously, would add subtle emphasis by stressing or underplaying that part of the design. Leads were even realistically milled to represent branches, tree-trunks, and, as in one window in the McKean collection, butterflies. No effect was too trivial, too difficult to achieve.

A contemporary anonymous article in *The World's Work* describes this attention to detail: "in the new system, the leads are treated as parts of the picture. For instance, in a piece of foliage the lead represents the twigs and stems, and is made thick and rough to indicate the wood, or in representing drapery it follows the seams of the fabric. This produces a new effect not before obtained in stained glass. Seen at night, with a light inside the window, stained glass is usually a confused mass of lines, representing nothing. In the new method, the leads actually represent the outlines of the picture, and the window has an increased decorative value."

The early heavy leading of the 1880s was replaced by 1900 with thin, neat lines, sometimes patinated in gold or silver. In 1905 the Studios announced a new development: a window "without reinforcing bars." The glass was braced with narrow steel rods soldered on to the lead lines on the back of the window, thereby eliminating the need for the heavy and unsightly bars which by tradition had been placed at regular intervals across the window to provide support.

Tiffany continued to experiment: as late as 1912 he designed the "Angel of Truth" Shedd Memorial window to do away with all conventional reinforcing, both leads and cross bars –

the manner in which the painted sections of glass were plated providing the necessary structural support.

Special effects: Where Tiffany's rules were not actually broken, they were considerably bent. The Studios' booklets boasted that its windows contained no paint, yet the most enchanting effects were obtained by dabbing splashes of yellow or red enamel in the centre of flowers to heighten the overall effect. The enamel was usually painted on the back of the piece of glass and then concealed within a second plated piece, leaving the curious viewer with the impression that the effect must be *in* the glass rather than *on the back* of it. On rare occasions the rules were waived so drastically that one wonders whether Tiffany was aware of the event. The "Desert Scout" Goodrich Memorial in Lakewood cemetery, Minneapolis, for example, consists of a large double layer of sheet glass on which all the detail is etched and painted in heavy bright enamels. There are no lead lines at all. The window is so out of character with what one associates with the firm's work that it is difficult to imagine the circumstances surrounding the commission. An almost identical window in the Church of the Holy Redeemer, Bryn Mawr, Pa., is similarly atypical.

Edward E. Hayward, an employee at Tiffany Studios for fifty years, later recalled another occasion on which convention was broken, this time with Tiffany's reluctant complicity. The First Presbyterian Church in Pittsburgh commissioned a series of painted windows in Cathedral glass backed with an opalescent layer. Tiffany stipulated that the contract specifically mention that this was contrary to his philosophies as a founder-member of the American School of Stained Glass. If he was to be party to a breach of ideals, a record had to be kept so that history could exonerate him.

Faults: Tiffany's windows, incomparable though they were in so many ways, did have certain technical faults. The main problem, ironically, concerned the use of the very enamel paints which had initially spurred Tiffany to create a type of glass that would entirely eliminate the need for them. The painted areas on Tiffany windows – limited in most instances to the face and hands – were executed in flesh-colored enamels. These, on being fired, did not always vitrify completely, with the result that the paint, exposed to the temperature fluctuations of summer and winter, would sometimes peel. In extreme cases no paint has survived. Examples of severe deterioration can be seen in St. Stephen's Episcopal Church, Providence; Trinity Church, New Haven; the First Reformed Dutch Church, Brooklyn; and in numerous mausoleums.

Two other technical problems have evolved through the years from Tiffany's use of plating. The first is that the accumulated weight of the layers of glass has brought enormous pressure to bear on the lower sections of large windows. Severe buckling and cracking have often occurred, as in the chancel window at St. Mark's in Washington, D.C. Secondly, dirt and condensation have sometimes worked their way between the layers, turning back the light on its path through the window and decaying the wood frame.

International exhibitions

"Feeding the Flamingoes," the watercolor painted by Tiffany in 1885 that became the cartoon for the matching window at the 1893 Chicago Columbian Exposition. The window, which was later installed in Laurelton Hall (see p. 161), was described in the Tiffany exposition booklet as "more realistic, more elaborate, and showing more clearly the possibilities of American glass than any window in our exhibit." It is now in the McKean collection.

HE LAST YEARS OF THE nineteenth century provided aspiring artists with numerous international expositions which could help them to expand their reputations to match their ambitions. Tiffany, although firmly established within America by 1890, was still largely unknown in Europe. The next ten years would dramatically change all that, to the point that after 1900 he felt – certainly as concerned his windows – that further exposure was superfluous.

Tiffany's first major challenge was afforded by the 1893 Columbian Exposition in Chicago. Here, at exactly the right moment, was the international platform on which his windows would dazzle the world and finally extinguish the lingering European doubt of the merits of his revolution in stained glass. Tiffany was supremely confident, even advocating a special gallery in which *all* American windows would be displayed side by side for comparative judgment. When this request was denied, he wrote that "you will look in vain in the great 'White City' on the shores of Lake Michigan for a department in the Exposition devoted exclusively to exhibiting the results of the development in this particular art. This is more to be regretted as in a new art, such as this, exhibitions are of great use; the artist comes face to face with his fellow artists, and patrons are better able to judge of the merits of the work of each." Alternative space was provided for Tiffany in a section of the Manufacturers and Liberal Arts Building which his father had reserved for the Tiffany & Company exhibit.

The booklet which Tiffany Studios published on their exhibit described the remarkable range of items, a range carefully balanced to cover the entire gamut of domestic and ecclesiastical decoration – frescoes, murals, stained glass windows, marble and glass mosaics, wood carvings, metal work, embroideries, upholsteries, and tapestries. There were three main display areas: a Dark Room, Light Room, and, replete with an example of every liturgical object, Tiffany's sumptuous Romanesque Chapel. Each area contained windows, some of which are illustrated here. Also displayed was a semicircular memorial by Will Low, a triptych of "Christ Blessing St. John" by Frederick Wilson, and a window modelled on Botticelli's "Madonna and Child." Unfortunately, no complete list of Exposition windows was published, so complete identification is impossible.

The Chapel, subsequently purchased by Mrs. Celia Whipple Wallace of Chicago for $50,000 and donated to the Cathedral of St. John the Divine on Morningside Heights in New York, put the stamp on Tiffany's genius. Over one million visitors filed through its doors to gaze in awe at the series of windows, mosaics, sanctuary lamps, jewel-encrusted altar, tabernacle and crucifix. Although the gaudy neo-Byzantine decorations were considered by most critics as over-ripe and grossly overplayed, Tiffany's intentions were seen as a sincere search for a new beginning. He had placed himself in declared opposition to all that was traditional and stereotyped within the arts. Wilhelm von Bode, the Director of the Gemäldegalerie in Berlin, was lavish in his praise, especially for the windows which he found "of a perfection which allows them to be placed alongside the products of antiquity or the Middle Ages." He concluded that they received far more attention at the Fair than any other product of American industrial art. Others who were equally enthusiastic were the critics André Bouilhet, Julius Lessing, and Samuel Bing, whose association with Tiffany is described below.

The Jury at the Exposition provided the official seal of approval, presenting Tiffany with an unprecedented 54 awards.

Samuel Bing played the principal role in bringing Tiffany's work and, finally, his fame to Europe. On moving to Paris from his native Hamburg in 1871, Bing established himself as an Oriental art dealer par excellence at a shop at 22 rue de Provence. In the late 1880s business had expanded to the point

"The Entombment," designed by Tiffany for the Chapel which he exhibited at the 1893 Columbian Exposition in Chicago. The Chapel was subsequently purchased by Mrs. Celia W. Wallace and installed in the Cathedral of St. John the Divine, New York, from where it was transferred to Laurelton Hall. The window is now in the McKean collection.

(*Above right*) "The Head of Joseph of Arimathea," designed by Tiffany. It is a reproduction of the Saint's head in "The Entombment" window which was exhibited at the 1893 exhibition in Chicago. "The Entombment" was a Memorial to Tiffany's father and therefore supports the belief that the head was modelled on Charles Lewis Tiffany. This panel was exhibited at the 1899 Grafton Galleries exhibition in London and later installed in Laurelton Hall. The study was also reproduced as a mosaic panel which was displayed on the stairway at the Tiffany Studios' showroom on Madison Avenue.

where he could open a branch on Fifth Avenue, New York, where he was introduced to the work of Tiffany, La Farge, Edward C. Moore (a partner in Charles L. Tiffany's silver firm), and Samuel Coleman. All were engaged in some branch of the industrial arts and Bing was greatly impressed by what he saw as a significant new departure within the arts. No doubt wishing to examine this more closely, he accepted an assignment in 1893 from Henri Roujon, the Director of the Beaux-Arts in Paris, to investigate the level of the decorative and industrial arts in the United States. His report, *La Culture artistique en Amérique*, was published in 1896. The highest accolades were reserved for Tiffany, whom Bing singled out as the most important force in American art at that time.

On returning to Paris in 1894, Bing immediately acted on the ideas which had taken root during his trip. He was perfectly placed to launch the parallel industrial arts movement which would soon be under way in France. Numerous decorators and artists were retained to convert his shop from an Oriental gallery into a *Salon de l'Art Nouveau*, and advertisements were placed in Parisian periodicals to invite artists to exhibit through him. Further invitations were extended to international artists to participate in the official opening on December 26th, 1895.

Included within the galleries of paintings, sculpture, jewelry, blown glass and furniture were ten windows designed by nine young French painters and executed by Tiffany in New York. Bing clearly saw himself as a link between the French window designer and the American stained glass craftsman, bringing them together for mutual benefit. He felt that the former could not have his works carried out effectively in France (due to the decline of the stained glass industry there) and the latter, i.e., Tiffany, could not dispense with the individuality of style which characterized the young Frenchmen. Bing chose as his designers the group of painters known as the "Nabis," who claimed that their works represented the art of the future ("Nabi" is the Hebraic word for "Prophet"). Included were such promising artists as Bonnard, Denis, Vuillard, Roussel, and Ibels. The windows were completed by Tiffany and shipped to Paris in time to be exhibited at the annual Salon du Champ-de-Mars prior to installation in Bing's shop.

The two lists below are taken from the respective catalogues for the exhibitions at the Champ-de-Mars and Bing's shop. It is curious that only seven of the ten shown on each occasion were common to *both*. Windows by Grasset, Serusier, and the second one by Ranson at the Champ-de-Mars were replaced by works by Denis, Isaac, and Besnard. No explanation for this switch was given.

Salon du Champ-de-Mars	*Salon de l'Art Nouveau Bing*
(SHOWN AT BOTH)	
La Moisson fleurie by Paul Ranson	
Le Jardin by Roussel	
La Maternité by Pierre Bonnard	
L'Eté by Ibels	
Les Marronniers by Vuillard	
Papa Chrysanthème by Toulouse Lautrec	
Parisiennes by Félix Vallotton	
Musique d'Automne by Eugène Grasset	*Un Paysage* by Maurice Denis
8 panels by P. Serusier	*Iris et Roseaux* by P.-A. Isaacs
a panel surmounting a dining-room chimney by Paul Ranson	*La Cascade* by Albert Besnard

"La Moisson Fleurie" ("harvest in bloom"), one of two windows designed by Paul Ranson which were displayed in 1895 at both the *Salon* of the Champ-de-Mars and Bing's shop at 22 rue de Provence, Paris.

Edouard Vuillard's cartoon for "Les Marronniers" ("The chestnut trees"), a Tiffany window which was exhibited at both the 1895 Champ-de-Mars *Salon* and at Bing's shop. The cartoon was purchased in 1909 from Bing by the Bernheim-Jeune Gallery.

Bonnard exhibited this cartoon for the "Maternité" window at the 1895 *Salon* of the Société des Beaux-Arts. It was purchased from Bing by the Bernheim-Jeune Gallery in 1909. (*Photo courtesy of Bernheim-Jeune Gallery*)

"La Maternité," designed by Pierre Bonnard and exhibited at both the *Salon* of the Champ-de-Mars and Bing's shop in 1895.

Reaction to the windows was mixed. The critic Roger Marx found that "Mr. Tiffany displays a series of windows which show to maximum advantage, and with proven ingenuity, that American glass has qualities which match the richness of precious hardstones, jades, and marble." Another critic, in the *Revue des Arts Décoratifs*, was equally enthusiastic. He wrote, "One knows with what success the Americans have addressed themselves to the art of window-making. Their work in this art form has achieved a very real originality."

Most of the criticism was negative, however. The mildest comment came from René de Cuers, who conceded that, "while they are not beautiful in the absolute meaning of the word, they are certainly interesting on several grounds." He found Roussel's *Le Jardin* very primitive, "the artlessness of the impression felt makes one smile and forgive." The two by Ibels and Lautrec he described as "curious landscapes fantastical to a degree, only of very relative interest. It would be unwise

"Le Jardin," the window designed ▷
by Ker-Xavier Roussel and
exhibited in 1895 at both the *Salon*
of the Champ-de-Mars and Bing's
shop. The cartoon is in the
Carnegie Institute, Pittsburgh (see
Carnegie Magazine, December
1978, pp. 17–19).

"L'Eté," the window designed by
Henri-Guillaume Ibels which was
exhibited in 1895 at the Champ-
de-Mars *Salon* and at Bing's shop.

"Papa Chrysanthème," the   ▷
window designed by Toulouse-
Lautrec and exhibited in 1895 at
the *Salon* of the Champ-de-Mars
and at Bing's shop. It is now in the
Collection of the Musées
Nationaux, Paris.

"Parisiennes," designed by Félix Vallotton and shown in 1895 at both the Champ-de-Mars and Bing's shop. Bing later included it in his exhibit at the 1902 Turin World Exposition.

(*Far right*) "La Cascade," the window designed by A. Besnard and exhibited at the 1895 *Salon* of the Champ-de-Mars.

(*Below*) The "Deep Sea" window designed by Tiffany and exhibited at the *Libre Esthétique*, Brussels, in 1897. Cecilia Waern described the window in *Studio International* as "a great favorite of mine, and indeed of all European critics who see it, for its subdued depth of color and poetic suggestiveness."

on our part to make any great effort to fathom the allegory of these productions; not only would it be a tough task, but one would run a serious risk of not correctly interpreting the artist's idea. We leave full latitude to our reader's imagination." Léon de Fourcaud, in an article on the Champ-de-Mars exhibition in which he described a window by La Farge as a "dazzling bouquet of peonies," referred to the Nabis' windows as "ce bizarre manifeste." Clearly, Bing's "new art" was still too new.

Another important international forum was provided by the exhibition which Bing held at the Grafton Galleries in London in 1899. Of all Bing's commissioned artists – for example, Colonna, Meunier, Lalique, and Gallé – Tiffany was the most lavishly represented, to such a degree that the critic Horace Townsend wrote, "Never before has so extensive an exhibit as this been made, Mr. Tiffany having stripped his studios and store houses bare in order to more fully and thoroughly represent himself in English eyes." The cabinets were crammed with Favrile vases decorated with his most recent innovations: the iridescent peacock feather motif and reticulated bronze mounts. Townsend was filled "first with amazement and eventually with bewilderment." The windows, interspaced with the cabinets, were awash with color, presenting a stark challenge to the mediocrity of English stained glass from the heart of the enemy camp.

84 The landscape window at Temple Emmanuel,
Fifth Avenue, New York. Installed in the Beth-El
chapel, it depicts Moses' tablets flanked by Solomon's
Temple on Mount Zion.

85 The Mitteldorfer Memorial window in the Beth
Ahabah Congregation, Richmond, Va.

88 "Lilies and Apple Blossoms," the Julia Wheeler ▷
Tiffany Memorial in the St. James Episcopal Church,
Fordham, New York. Mrs. Tiffany was the wife of
the third Rector of the parish.

86   A tropical landscape window. (*Photo: courtesy
Dr. Egon Neustadt*)

87   A domestic window depicting a wishing well
and picket fence. (*Photo: courtesy Dr. Egon Neustadt*)

In Tender
and Reverent
Memory ✠ of
Julia Wheeler Tiffany

89 "Flower, Fish, and Fruit," designed by Tiffany in 1885 for Miss Mary Elizabeth Garrett's Baltimore home, where it was installed as part of the transom in the dining-room. Clearly a favorite early commission, Tiffany displayed the original cartoon at the 1899 Grafton Gallery exhibition in London and later made a duplicate window which he installed in Laurelton Hall (see p. 161). Miss Garrett's window is illustrated in C. Dekay, *The Art Work of Louis C. Tiffany*, New York 1914, opp. p. 16. It is now in the Baltimore Museum of Art.

90 A domestic floral window of trellised trumpet vines (*courtesy of Ohio Antiques*).

91 A passion flower floral window. (*Photo:* ▷ *courtesy Dr. Egon Neustadt*)

92　A grape arbor window with trellised blue grape clusters.

93　This magnolia and apple blossom window was commissioned by George E. Dimock for his house in Elizabeth, New Jersey. It is now in the Virginia Museum of Art, Richmond.

94　The "Morning Glories" Memorial ▷ in the Unitarian Church, Northampton, Mass., *c.* 1905.

95　The "Autumn Leaves" Memorial to Joseph and Anne Dean Lyman in the Unitarian Church, Northampton, Mass., *c.* 1905.

AND WITH THE MORN
THOSE ANGEL FACES
SMILE WHICH WE HAVE

LOVED LONG SINCE
AND LOST AWHILE

THE : MEMORIAL
OF:VIRTUE :IS: IM-
MORTAL: BECAUSE

IT:IS:KNOWN:WITH
GOD:AND:WITH:MEN

96 This domestic window incorporates two favorite Tiffany themes: the snowball and wisteria. Part of the Gluck collection which was offered at Christie's on February 17th, 1979, it sold for $52,800.

97 This skylight window was commissioned by Curtis Q. McWilliams, founder of the Public Water Supply Company in Shamokin, Pa., in 1914. The cost, including a set of clear transom windows, was $1,199.78. The window was installed horizontally above a stairway. Each of the panels is slightly bowed, presumably to simulate pendant boughs. The window was sold at Christie's in May, 1978, for $60,500, a world record for a Tiffany window.

98 A magnolia panel taken some years ago from its original setting in a New Orleans house (private collection).

100 This skylight window depicts
clematis and trumpet vines, *c.* 1920. The
corners open upwards to allow for
ventilation or changing light bulbs. ▷

99 A domestic panel with parrots
perched among hibiscus. (*Photo:
Earl Sydnor*)

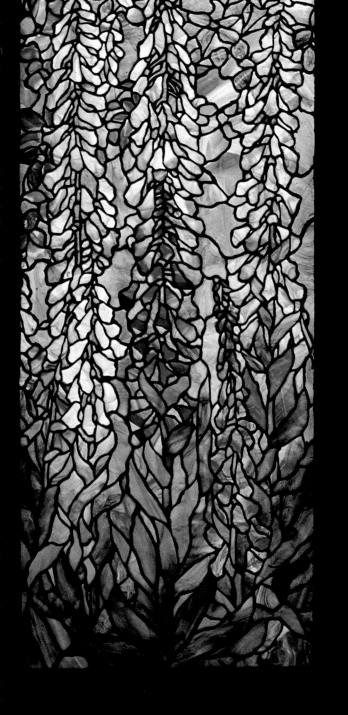

◁ 101　The Cyrus H.
McCormick windows
in St. Mary's Episcopal
Church, Pacific Grove,
California, 1922. They
depict foxgloves and
Easter lilies beneath
clematis.

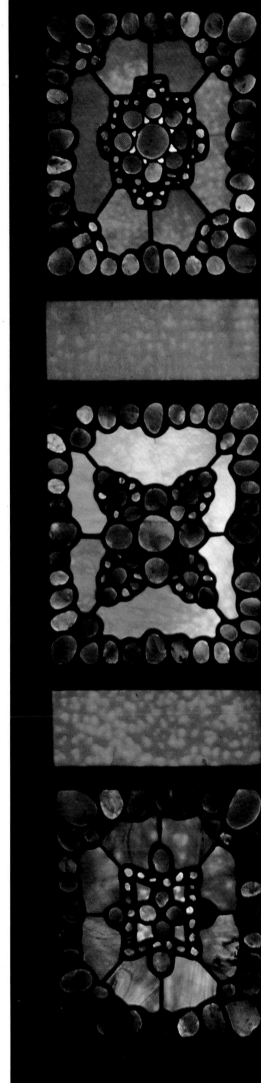

102　A set of six glass
and pebble-cluster
panels incorporated into
a single window
(private collection).

◁ 103   The Clara A. Geer Memorial
medallion window in the Christ
Episcopal Church, Rye, New York,
1914. The window provides a delightful
variation on the standard medallion
model.

104   "I am the Vine. Ye are the
Branches." One of two jewelled
medallion windows in the First
Unitarian Church, Fairfield, Conn.

105 "Rose Window," a domestic window of ornamental floral design made in 1906 for general exhibition purposes and later installed on the stair landing at Laurelton Hall. Illustrated in *The Art Work of L. C. Tiffany*, it is now in the McKean Collection.

106 One of two identical pebble-cluster panels in Maxwell Plum's restaurant, New York City. The flowers in the central medallion have pebble petals with glass centers.

The exhibition catalogue lists the following Tiffany
windows and cartoons:

WINDOWS

1 Fish
2 Peonies
3 Italian Garden, from a cartoon by L. C. Tiffany
4 Upper section of # 10
5 Sheet of Favrile Glass with quartz pebbles
6 "Music," from a cartoon by Frank Brangwyn
6a "The Fire Worshippers," from a cartoon by F. S. Church
7 Ornamental panel
8 Fish
9 "Baptism of Christ," from a cartoon by Frank Brangwyn
10 Window in memory of Edward T. Steel, former superintendent
    of Schools, Philadelphia, from a cartoon by Frederick Wilson
11 In the style of a Chartres Window of the Twelfth Century
12 Eggplant
13 "Head of Joseph of Arimathea," from "The Entombment," a
    window of L. C. Tiffany exhibited at the World's Fair in Chicago,
    now in the Cathedral of St. John the Divine, New York City

CARTOONS & SKETCHES

1 Windows and mosaic in the Church of St. Michael and All
    Angels, New York City. The five central panels are windows and
    those at either end are in mosaic
2 A collection of sketches for windows, decorations, mosaics, etc.

The exhibition was a resounding success, both reinforcing
Tiffany's international status and providing a dress rehearsal
for the following year's World Exposition in Paris.

The 1900 *Exposition Universelle* was the last international
exhibition in which Tiffany seriously promoted his windows.
Thereafter, in St. Petersburg and Dresden in 1901, in Turin in
1902, and in St. Louis in 1904, the emphasis shifted to his
Favrile vases and, increasingly, to his lamps. Perhaps Tiffany
felt that, after the exhilarating experimentation of the 1890s,

Brangwyn's cartoon for the window entitled "Girl Picking Gourds," which was executed in the 1890s and later installed by Tiffany in the living room at Laurelton Hall (see p. 161). The window is now in the McKean collection. (*Photo courtesy of Musée des Décoratifs, Paris*)

"Nymphs and Satyr," designed by Frank Brangwyn and exhibited at the 1899 Grafton Galleries exhibition. It was illustrated in *The Decorative Art of Frank Brangwyn*, London, 1924, p. 192; see also *Dekorative Kunst*, 1899, p. 122.

"Music," the cartoon for the Brangwyn window which Tiffany exhibited at the Grafton Galleries in 1899.

there was no new ground to break in window design or technique. One of his major windows at the 1900 Exposition, in fact, was "The Four Seasons" which had been shown in Paris eight years earlier. It was placed to the left of the entrance to the United States pavilion and was matched, on the right-hand side, by the religious window which was later installed in the Wade Chapel at Lakeview cemetery, Cleveland. Inside, the Tiffany exhibit offered the predictably wide selection of recent glassware, though there were noticeably fewer examples of windows than in previous expositions of this calibre. One, a small panel of hydrangeas in deeply mottled and fractured glass, was bought by a Mrs. Ingrid Kiaer from Oslo. Most of the others appear to have been the perennial favorites used for exhibition purposes only. The Jury awarded Tiffany a Grand Prix for his glassware, not his windows. Clearly, they felt that this was the avenue along which he had recently progressed the furthest.

SPRING
SUMMER
WINTER
ANNO
DOMINI
MDCCC

"The Four Seasons" was designed by Tiffany to demonstrate the beauty of Favrile glass. It was exhibited in 1892 in London and Paris and again at the 1900 Exposition Universelle in Paris, where it was displayed on one side of the entrance to the United States pavilion. Tiffany later installed the four panels separately in an alcove at Laurelton Hall (see p. 161) and placed the eagle frieze over the main entrance door. All parts of the window are now in the McKean collection.

Window themes

a Figure windows: religious

THE BULK OF THE STUDIOS' WORK was provided by commissions for ecclesiastical figure windows. Congregationalists within the Presbyterian Church, especially, ordered a seemingly unlimited stream of commissions for memorials in glass. Pictorial representation of all major Old and New Testament stories was sought. Some, such as "Christ Blessing Little Children" and "The Ascension," proved perennial favorites. Tiffany naturally catered to this market, publishing several booklets to promote it. What better way to pay one's respects to a dearly departed relative or church rector than to commission a Biblical window in which scenes from the life of Christ or His Apostles were portrayed? What more fitting memorial to a young mother than "The Nativity" or "Christ the Good Shepherd" for a faithful pastor? Every page of Holy Writ is filled with thoughts that could be readily adapted into Church window iconography. Outstanding examples abound: the "Celestial Hierarchy" chancel window in St. Michael's Episcopal Church on Amsterdam Avenue in New York City consists of five panels flanked by matching mosaic friezes which depict St. Michael amongst adoring angels and choristers. The nearby All Angels' Church on West End Avenue (now demolished) contained twelve lancet windows portraying the major events in Christ's life from His birth to His resurrection. Alternatively, the allegorical figure of "Hope" or "Truth," standing proudly in a field of Easter lilies, would prove a most fitting tribute.

Local color was provided in several instances by incorporating the church's minister or members of the congregation into the window. The faces of the crowd in the "Christ Leaving the Praetorium" window in St. Paul's, Milwaukee (1888), are those of the congregation, while the "Moses" in the Lafayette Avenue Presbyterian Church in Brooklyn is the first rector, Dr. Cuyler.

"Christ Blessing Children," the Bodine Memorial in the First Methodist Church, Germantown, Pa.

"Christ Knocking at the Door," the John Patterson Coyle Memorial in the First Congregational Church, North Adams, Mass., c. 1898. One of the most popular themes for religious windows, the present example is one of the most successful.

"Christ and Nicodemus," the Judge Thomas Ewing Memorial window in the Third Presbyterian Church, Pittsburgh, which was donated by Mrs. G.E. Shaw, *c.* 1898.

"Joshua," the Sandham
Memorial in the Marble
Collegiate Church, New York
City. Joshua is shown raising his
hand to thank the Lord for
extending the day to allow him
and his Gideonite allies time to
defeat the Amorites (Joshua X:
13, 14).

(*Facing page*) An unidentified
Memorial window. The glass
plate from which this illustration
was taken was found at
Laurelton Hall in the 1950s.

"St. Mark," installed in the Episcopal Church, Islip, New York, in 1878. In *The Art Work of Louis C. Tiffany*, 1914, the window is described as "the first Tiffany window in American glass in combination with antique glass."

(*Far right*) "The Madonna of the Blossoms," designed by Frederick Wilson for the Arlington Street Church, Boston, *c.* 1898.

"The Valiant Woman," the Stillman Memorial in the Church of the Pilgrims, Brooklyn. Illustrated in several Studios publications and *The Arts of the Tiffanys*, 1914, the window is believed to have been destroyed when the Church was torn down some years ago.

"The Good Shepherd," the
Hensel Memorial in the Bryn
Mawr Presbyterian Church, Pa.

◁ "Christ Teaching by the Sea," the Welch Triptych Memorial in the First Methodist Church, Germantown, Pa.

"King David," the Stanwood Memorial in the First Congregational Church (now the South Parish Congregational) in Augusta, Maine. The strings on the harp are thin iron rods soldered on to the front of the window, an unusual technique for Tiffany.

"The Angel of Truth," the central panel of the John G. Shedd triptych Memorial in the Rosehill Cemetery Community mausoleum, Chicago. Installed *c.* 1912, the window drew comment for its lack of conventional reinforcing. The window was illustrated in *The New York Herald Magazine*, December 26th, 1915, p. 12.

◁ "Saint Paul Preaching at Athens," a Memorial window in St. Paul's Episcopal Church, Rochester, New York.

"The Angels of the Elements," the Martha Anderson Brown Memorial window in the Second Reformed Church, Hackensack, New Jersey. The four winged figures depict earth, air, fire and water.

To the Glory of God
and in loving memory of
Katharine Kelso Johnston
Wife of James Pemberton Hutchinson

and eldest daughter of
Alexander Johnston
and Lois Buchanan Cassatt
Born July 30, 1871 – Died April 11, 1903

(*Facing page*) (Left) "The Education of the Virgin," the Katherine Johnston Memorial in the Third Presbyterian Church, Germantown, Pa., *c.* 1905. (Right) "St. Agnes," the Lois Buchanan Cassatt Memorial in the Third Presbyterian Church, Germantown, Pa., *c.* 1905.

"Three Wise Men," a Memorial window now in a private collection. Its original location is unknown.

"The Good Shepherd," in Jersey City, New Jersey.

147

APRIL TWENTY-FIFTH MDCXXXVIII

b Figure windows: historical, mythological, and portrait

These encompassed a wide range of non-ecclesiastical commissions for universities, libraries, schools, hospitals, and private clients. The subject-matter matched the institution. Allegorical figures representing the various components of "Education" were depicted in Yale's Chittenden Library; the Alexander Commencement Hall at Princeton includes four rose windows symbolizing "Knowledge," "Fame," "Genius," and "Study;" the Packer Institute in Brooklyn portrays Dante, Virgil, and Beatrice; "Art and Literature" was the theme chosen for the Tilton Memorial Library at Tulane, New Orleans; Themistocles and Aristides stare sternly down on undergraduates registering in Harvard's Memorial Hall; the Hartford Hospital chose a robed figure of Æsculapius to inspire its Hippocratic oath.

Elsewhere, "Motherhood and Music" was commissioned for the Lake Erie Women's College in Painesville, Ohio, while "King Alfred and Sir Galahad" was the theme for a window at St. Mark's School in Southboro, Mass. Moments in American colonial history also inspired commissions; these, predictably, mainly in New England.

A number of portrait windows were likewise undertaken for private clients. Joseph Delamar, for example, commissioned a window of his wife, Nellie Virginia Sands, clad in Grecian robes beneath pendant wisteria. Most of these windows, however, remain unrecorded, often reappearing on today's market with no identification of whom they represent. One removed from the Mellon house in Pittsburgh shows a young woman, presumably a daughter, with a raised garland of flowers.

The Morse Gallery in Winter Park, Florida, contains three fine early figure windows: Tiffany's "Feeding the Flamingoes," "Girl Picking Gourds" (from a Brangwyn cartoon), and "Young Woman at a Fountain" (from Will Low's *Aurora*). The last-mentioned achieves a brilliantly realistic impression of falling water by the placement of a thin strip of translucent rippled blue glass between adjoining sections which are heavily plated on the back to prevent the sunlight from penetrating to the same degree that it does where the water flows into the fountain.

"The Hector," the T.R. Trowbridge Memorial installed in the First Church of Christ, New Haven, 1898. The Hector was the ship which brought the early colonists to New Haven in 1638. The corners of the window depict the church congregation's four meeting houses, dated 1640, 1670, 1757, and 1814. When the church was restored to its original early nineteenth-century architectural style in the 1960s, the window was donated to the Southern Connecticut State College.

"Alcuin and Charlemagne," the cartoon by Frederick Wilson for one of two windows installed in the Chapel at LaFayette College in Easton, Pa., c. 1893. Both were destroyed when the Chapel was gutted by fire. Alcuin was the English man-of-letters who assisted Charlemagne in founding a royal academy.

"Mather addressing the British Commission," the George Henry Eager Memorial window installed in the Second Unitarian Church in Boston, 1899. Increase Mather is depicted protesting the surrender of the Colony charter to the English Commissioners, 1683–84. The Second Unitarian Church has now merged with the First Church, the latter having previously been ravaged by fire.

"Antony van Corlear, the Trumpeter of New Amsterdam," the Tiffany stairway window designed by Howard Pyle for the Colonial Club at Broadway and 72nd Street, New York. The building was torn down some years ago.

An early window depicting Peter Stuyvesant, the Governor of New Amsterdam, as New York was then known. Now in a private collection, it is possible that the window was initially installed in the Stuyvesant Theater in New York which was demolished many years ago.

"Recreation and Music," the Thompson Memorial window designed by
Frederick Wilson and installed in the Postgraduate Hospital in New York City
in 1899.

"Sir Galahad," the Ogden Cryder Memorial in St. Andrew's Dune Church, ▷
Southampton, N.Y., 1902.

This triptych Memorial was commissioned by the Women's Relief Corps of the North and the United Daughters of the Confederacy of the South for the National Headquarters of the American Red Cross, Washington, D.C. The left-hand panel depicts St. Filomena accompanied by figures representing Mercy, Hope, Faith, and Charity; in the centre a Red Cross knight administers aid to a wounded comrade; the right-hand panel depicts Una of Spenser's "Faerie Queene" and symbolizes Truth.

This sketch depicts Sir Galahad sustained by the Holy Grail while confined in prison. It was illustrated as a suggestion for a Memorial window in *Tributes to Honor*, published by the Studios' Ecclesiastical Department.

An unidentified domestic figure window illustrated in a French decorative arts magazine in 1904. It is interesting to compare the window with that in the Wayne Community College (see color plate 31): the central two figures have been incorporated into both with minor differences. (*Photo courtesy of Musée des Arts Décoratifs, Paris*)

An unidentified figure window. The glass plate from which this illustration was ▷ made was discovered at Laurelton Hall in the 1950s.

This cartoon for a triptych entitled "A Spring Scene" was designed by Tiffany for the residence of Mr. William A. Slater of Norwich, Conn. It was illustrated in Will H. Low, "Old Glass in New Windows," *Scribner's Magazine*, IV, 1888, p. 678.

"The Four Seasons," commissioned by Walter Jennings for his country residence. The top half depicts Spring and Summer, the bottom Autumn and Winter.

"Music," one of the twelve Steel Memorial windows depicting "Education" designed by Frederick Wilson for the New Philadelphia High School, Philadelphia. The set, comprising Agriculture, Astronomy, Joinery, Sewing, Recreation, Architecture, Painting, Music, Chemistry, Cooking, Study, and Forging, was exhibited at the 1899 Grafton Galleries exhibition in London.

This landscape window was illustrated in *The Arts of the Tiffanys*, 1914.

"Autumn," designed by Lydia Emmet and exhibited at the 1893 Chicago Columbian Exposition. Tiffany later installed the window in the house which he decorated for Samuel Clements (Mark Twain) at Nook Farm, Hartford, Conn. When the house was sold in 1902, the new owner had it removed. Its whereabouts are unknown.

"Twilight," the large triptych designed by Tiffany for Linden Hall, the home of Sarah Cochran, a coal baroness in Dawson, Pa., but installed in her Pittsburgh house. The window is illustrated in *Munsey's Magazine*, December, 1902, p. 394.

A corner of the living room at Laurelton Hall, *c.* 1914. It represents a gallery of Tiffany's favorite windows, most of which he had designed in the early years for exhibition purposes or for top clients and which he either retained or re-acquired. In the centre is "The Bathers." In the top row, from the left, are "Fish and Fruit" (a duplicate of the window designed for Miss E. Garrett in 1888), and the "Four Seasons" panels: Spring, Summer, Autumn and Winter. Beneath them are "Feeding the Flamingoes," the "Eggplant" window, and, partly obscured on the right, "Girl Picking Gourds."

c Landscape windows

These, more than any other single facet of his work, bear the stamp of Tiffany's mastery of stained glass. Nothing else is so identifiable, so arresting in its beauty or impact. Drawing, as one biographer wrote, from "the endless wealth of precept and suggestion that lies around us in air and water and earth, in all the vast teeming bosom of Nature," Tiffany set out not only to capture the out of doors in its many moods, but to improve on it. Can one recall looking out across such a perfectly symmetrical dusk landscape with central meandering stream flanked by mossy banks carpeted with flowers in a riot of blues and yellows? Never was Nature's palette so radiant, so shot through with color. Commissions poured in.

Criticism was sometimes voiced by church elders of the suitability of a memorial window which did not depict a scene from the Scriptures. Religious windows were by tradition pictorial, to educate and elevate the congregation. Tiffany circumvented this by stressing the deeply religious symbolism of his landscapes. One was entitled, "Lift up thine eyes unto the hills from whence cometh your help;" others took their inspiration from the 24th Psalm and the 42th Psalm of David ("As the Hart panteth after the water brooks, so panteth my soul after Thee, O God"); others, again, provided a partial glimpse of Jerusalem through the clouds, being called "Holy City" or "Vision of St. John." Mausoleum landscape windows frequently portrayed "The River of Life" in which the stream flowing from the distant hills symbolized one's path from birth to death.

Tiffany interspersed these landscapes with favorite themes. Peacocks strut or perch on balustrades; dow-like boats sail on small stretches of rippled blue water; the pediment of a Greek temple is silhouetted against a setting sun. Everywhere there are trees; the birch most commonly in views of the New England countryside, the cypress in landscaped gardens. Frequently, the window was a direct translation into glass of the countryside neighboring the house. The Cole Memorial installed in the Aftenro Old Age Home in Duluth, for example, pictures the hills behind the town.

The landscape window commissioned by Mr. Towle and donated in 1925 to the Metropolitan Museum of Art by William de Forest.

A landscape Memorial window designed by Agnes Northrop.

"He Leadeth Me beside the Still Waters," the Louis Derr Memorial window designed by Agnes Northrop, *c.* 1900 (private collection).

An unidentified landscape window designed by Agnes Northrop.

A Memorial window designed by Agnes Northrop for a Midwestern mausoleum.

"THE IRIS AND FLOWERS YOU LOVED SO WELL BRING BACK SWEET MEMORIES OF YOU"

The landscape window commissioned by Andrew Carnegie for Dunfermline Abbey, Scotland, as a Memorial to his parents. Originally intended for the south wall in the nave, it is now in the adjoining Carnegie Hall. The dedicatory plaque reads "In loving memory of William Carnegie of Dunfermline, Margaret Morrison his wife, Ann and Thomas their children. Erected by their sole surviving son, 1913."

166

◁ This Memorial window was entitled "The Earth is the Lord's and the Fullness thereof." It was illustrated in a booklet by Ethel Syford on recent Tiffany works in 1911.

◁ A domestic landscape window depicting a view through a colonnade of a distant range of hills. The window was removed from a house in New Jersey some years ago. (Collection Stuart Pivar)

The Maria Louise Beebe Memorial in the Y.W.C.A. at 53rd Street and Lexington Avenue, New York, installed *c.* 1917.

"Sunrise" and "Sunset," a pair of Memorial windows commissioned in 1918 for a mausoleum in a New York cemetery and now in Henry Afrika's restaurant in San Francisco.

This photograph was found among Tiffany memorabilia at Laurelton Hall in the late 1950s. The whereabouts of the window are unknown.

The Edith and Edward Darling Memorial in the Bay Head Chapel, Bay Head, New Jersey, c. 1904.

The lower half of the landscape
window commissioned in 1910
by Miss Helen Gould for her
residence at 579 Fifth Avenue,
New York. The entire window
is illustrated in Ethel Syford,
*Examples of Recent Work from
the Studios of Louis C. Tiffany*,
Boston, 1911. It was designed
by Agnes Northrop.

"Fulfilment," one of five panels depicting the four seasons (the fifth panel is entitled "All the Seasons"), in the Battell Chapel, Church of Christ Congregational, Norfolk, Conn. Donated by Mrs. Carl Stoeckel, the panel represents "Autumn" and takes its theme from Jeremiah VIII: 20: "The Summer is ended, the harvest is past." (See color plate 80.)

The Edwin D. Field Memorial
window in the Pilgrim
Congregational Church, Duluth,
Minnesota, *c.* 1921.

(*Facing page*) A landscape Memorial window, *c.* 1925, depicting a view along a stream to distant hills.

The Marguerita Dennisson Memorial in the First Presbyterian Church, Germantown, Pa., 1920s.

The Lauriston Livingston Stone Memorial in the Third Presbyterian Church, Rochester, New York, depicting an autumnal landscape, 1920s.

Sunset and evening star,
And one clear call for me,
And may there be no moaning of the bar,
When I put out to sea.   Tennyson

The Lucien and Julia Barnes Memorial in the Pilgrim Congregational Church, Duluth, Minnesota, 1930.

◁ "Crossing the Bar," the Heth Lorton Memorial in St. James's Episcopal Church, Richmond, Va. The inscription reads, "I hope to see my Pilot face to face when I have crossed the Bar."

d Floral windows

Tiffany enthusiasts will immediately recognize the floral panels as two-dimensional variations on his lamps: magnolia, peonies, hydrangeas, and trumpet vines blossom in profusion in narthex, apse, and private home. Almost every species was brought to pulsating bloom, the Easter lily (to symbolize Resurrection) and iris proving the most frequent.

One of Tiffany's earliest floral commissions was the dining-room transoms for Miss Elizabeth Garrett in 1885; in 1892 "The Four Seasons" sealed his mastery of this stained glass art form. Later, skylights of trellised clematis and dogwood were installed above stairways to catch the sun's rays and delight the ascending viewer. Tiffany's own homes became galleries for his favorite blooms. A magnolia casement window was installed in the apartment at the corner of Madison Avenue and 72nd Street into which he moved in 1886. The windows at Laurelton Hall were likewise awash with flowers; white and green pendant hydrangeas surmounted the entrance door, while the dining-room was skirted on three sides by blue and purple clusters of wisteria. Elsewhere there are poppies in St. John's Episcopal Church, Jersey City; lilies in the First Baptist Church, Duluth, Minnesota; and daffodils and daisies in St. Paul's Protestant Church, Nantucket, Mass. Gorgeous laburnum and convolvuli flower unnoticed in mausoleums and crypts throughout America. Vegetables were less frequently portrayed. The squash, eggplant, and pumpkin panels in the McKean collection were early essays which were not enlarged upon commercially.

A bamboo panel. (*Photo courtesy of Christie's, New York*)

A floral window depicting
foxgloves beneath trellised
clematis. The original Studios'
photograph is in the Avery
Library at Columbia
University. The whereabouts of
the window is unknown.

A three-panel screen depicting trellised clematis, gourds, and grape vines.

Reproduction of a XIIIth Century Panel executed by

Louis C. Tiffany Studios
Stained Glass Windows
Mosaics, Indoor Memorials
Church Decorations
Monuments, Mausoleums
46 West Twenty-Third Street, New York City

e Medallion, ornamental, and abstract windows

An original Studios' photograph of a magnolia panel designed by Agnes Northrop. The back of the photograph is inscribed "Magnolia Macryphilla Americana Grandifola."

Medallion: Tiffany drew on thirteenth-century stained glass designs for his own range of medallion windows. A 1905 Studios booklet emphasized the increasing demand for this type of memorial as "particularly suited to the clerestory, transept, or great East Windows." Tiffany took as his point of departure the mosaic concept employed by the medieval glaziers. As he wrote in 1893, "The glass employed at this time was pot-metal, a kind in which the color permeates the entire mass. It was made in unequal thicknesses and was filled with bubbles and other imperfections which added greatly to its brilliancy by affording many points against which the sun's rays were broken . . . color effect was the one aim an artist of the period had in view." Tiffany juxtaposed reds, blues, and radiant yellows in glowing mosaics of broken color incorporated into overlapping geometric or arabesque designs. These were often further enhanced with prismatic jewels and "turtle-back" tiles bordering a central landscape or figure medallion.

Fine examples can be seen in the First Presbyterian Church in Dayton, Ohio, and in St. John's Episcopal Church, Elizabeth, New Jersey.

One of the medallion windows
in the First Church of Christ
Congregational, Fairfield, Conn.

This medallion window was
made for exhibition purposes,
c. 1892.

Ornamental: The 1910 *Partial List of Windows* includes a large number of ornamental commissions. Invariably the windows are unambitious in design; for example, a central garland of flowers or apostolic emblem on a latticed ground is set into a thin fretwork or guilloche border accentuated at each corner with a chunky glass jewel. At Tiffany Studios one got what one could afford, and low budgets brought lightly decorated geometric panels. Several, however, were charmingly conceived, as in the series installed in the Temple Beth Zion in Buffalo (later gutted by fire) and the heavily jewelled rose window in the New Presbyterian Church in Bath, New York. Another extraordinary example is the jewel-encrusted cover above the pulpit in the First Presbyterian Church, Brooklyn. More modest are the ceiling and dome in the Court of Appeals and the State House in Annapolis, and the ornamental windows in the Seventh Armory building in Manhattan.

Abstract windows: Tiffany's experiments in abstraction can be traced to the window which he had himself both designed and glazed by 1880 for his first New York home, the studio and apartment on the top floor of the Bella Apartments at 48 East 26th Street. The window, now in the Robert Koch collection, incorporates a deep amethyst serpentine motif on a multi-colored ground. It ranks as one of the most uncharacteristic surviving pieces of the artist's work – starkly abstract by today's standards, even – one that evolved from his unceasing search for happy accidents of color. As he later explained, "Those of us in America who began to experiment in glass were untrammelled by tradition, and were moved solely by a desire to produce a thing of beauty, irrespective of any rule, doctrine, or theory beyond that governing good taste and true artistic judgment. At first very little attention was paid to mere form. Color, and color only, was the end sought. Hence the first efforts were largely confined to increasing the field of color and producing glass that had gem-like qualities."

Tiffany must have realized also that a well-balanced color composition, however fortuitously conceived, has a subliminal impact on the viewer which, in turn, triggers an independent chain of emotions and thoughts.

Pebbles from the streams and beaches near Corona provided the inspiration for a later range of less abstract panels. The small stones, sometimes roughly chiselled on the underside to facilitate leading and to refract the light, were incorporated with glass of complementary colors into charming panels such as the one that Joseph Briggs installed in his home in the mid-1880s. A pair of similar pebble-cluster panels can be seen at Maxwell Plum's Restaurant in New York City. Another is illustrated in "Industrial Arts of America," *International Studio*, II, 1897, p. 161.

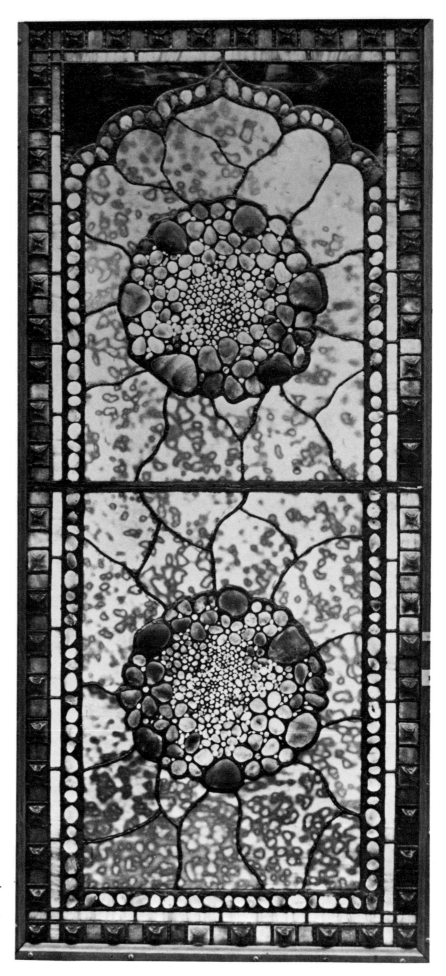

A "pebble–cluster" window,
c. 1885, incorporating central
medallions of pebbles bordered
by deeply mottled orange glass.
Several examples of this design
have survived. This one, which
was installed in Joseph Briggs's
house, is now in the McKean
Collection.

Signatures

IGNATURES first appeared on windows during the 1890s and continued into the 1920s, one in the Reformed Church, Hackensack, being dated as late as 1928. Yet not all were signed; the vast majority, in fact, were not. Nor can a distinction be made in this respect between important and lesser commissions; some of the windows which the Studios considered of major importance were not signed while several of its least inspired commissions bear a large enamelled firm's mark. The reason for this random method of identification is unclear. Unlike the lamp and desk-set models which were reproduced commercially in countless numbers with corresponding serial numbers, the windows were unique undertakings, each designed to meet a customer's specific wishes. The window took on this customer's identity; it became, for example, the *Taylor* or the *Stone* Memorial. Further identification seemed unnecessary as no duplicate window would be produced with which it might be confused. On occasion, no doubt, the client requested that the window be signed or the Studios itself decided that one of a series – as in certain church commissions – bear witness to Tiffany's work, but no clear pattern of signing is evident. The accompanying illustrations show how a window signature can help to date it chronologically.

Red enamel block capital lettering appears most frequently from 1900, replacing the black enamel capitals and lower case of the 1890s. Later, *circa* 1915, a script *L. C. Tiffany* signature became prevalent, often accompanied by the date. By the 1920s this script signature was invariably etched into the glass rather than enamelled on to its surface in pale blue, black and, rarely, mauve or green.

The signature is almost always found in the bottom right-hand corner of the window, although it was sometimes placed on the lower left-hand side. Infrequently, it appears on a small rectangle of glass which was plated on top of the window's surface, suggesting that the customer, on discovering that his commission was to be unsigned, made a late request that this be changed. I have seen bronze tags, such as those on Tiffany lamps, on a few windows, but in no instance did I feel that these were the original means of identification.

The most common form of signature found on windows between 1890 and 1899

An unusual signature from the same period, giving the year of the commission

The standard signature from 1900 to 1915. The firm's name was sometimes accompanied by the date

TIFFANY  STVDIOS

An unusual signature, *circa* 1905

The standard signature from *circa* 1915. Initially in black or red enamel, it was later etched on to the glass, sometimes with the date

Window chronology
Bibliography
Appendix

Window chronology

1875-77	Experiments at the Thill glasshouse in Brooklyn to eliminate the need to use paint on windows.
1877	Tiffany's first figure window, comprised of both European and American glass, in St. Mark's Episcopal Church, Islip, Long Island.
1878	Tiffany established his own glasshouse under the supervision of Andrea Boldini, of Venice. It burnt down, as did a second.
1879	The firm of L. C. Tiffany & Associated Artists formed with Samuel Coleman, Lockwood de Forest, and Candace Wheeler. Tiffany designed and executed an abstract window for his apartment in the Bella Apartments, New York.
1880–83	Continued experiments at the Louis Heidt glasshouse in Brooklyn.
1885	The Tiffany Glass Company Incorporated, New York City.
1886	Tiffany moved from the Bella Apartments into the upper floors of an apartment building on the N.W. corner of Madison Avenue at 72nd Street. Several windows were installed, including the triptych magnolia window now in the McKean collection.
1888	The Kempner Memorial entitled "Christ Leaving the Praetorium" installed in St. Paul's Episcopal Church, Milwaukee. This was Tiffany's largest figure window.
1890	The Tiffany Glass Company and L. C. Tiffany & Associated Artists merged into the Tiffany Glass & Decorating Company at 333–341 Fourth Avenue, Manhattan.
1892	The "Four Seasons" window exhibited in Paris.
1893	Tiffany's own glasshouse built at Corona, Long Island, with Arthur Nash, from Stourbridge, England, as Manager. Tiffany exhibited several windows and his Chapel at the Columbian Exposition in Chicago.
1895	Windows designed by French artists displayed at the *Salon du Champ-de-Mars* and Bing's *Salon de l'Art Nouveau* in Paris.
1899	The Chittenden Memorial, "Education," installed at Yale. Tiffany exhibit at the Grafton Galleries, London.
1900	Several windows exhibited at the *Exposition Universelle* in Paris.

The Tiffany Glass & Decorating Company became Tiffany Studios, at 347–355 Madison Avenue.

1902   The glasshouse at Corona renamed "Tiffany Furnaces."

1905   The Sage landscape Memorial installed in the First Presbyterian Church, Far Rockaway, Long Island.

1906   Laurelton Hall built at Cold Spring Harbor, Long Island. Several favorite windows were installed throughout the house.

1908–12   The landscape window installed in Richard B. Mellon's house in Pittsburgh.

1912   The peacock and cockatoo panels for Captain J. R. Delamar installed in his town house on Madison Avenue, New York.

1917   The Hartwell Memorial installed in the Central Baptist Church, Providence, Tiffany's largest landscape commission.

1924   Tiffany Furnaces closed. Later commissions utilized the excess glass which had accumulated through the years.

1932   Tiffany Studios filed for bankruptcy listing liabilities of $481,595 and assets of $315,907.

1933   L. C. Tiffany died on January 17th.

1930s   The Westminster Memorial Studios formed by former employees to complete outstanding Tiffany Studios commissions.

1978   World auction record of $60,500 for a Tiffany window at Christie's New York (see color plate 97).

Bibliography

"Angel of Truth for the John G. Shedd Mausoleum," *New York Herald Magazine*, 26 December 1915.

The Art of Louis Comfort Tiffany, The Toledo Museum of Art (exhibition catalogue), November–December, 1978

The Arts of Louis Comfort Tiffany and His Times, John and Mabel Ringling Museum of Art (exhibition catalogue), 1975

Bing, S. *Artistic America, Tiffany Glass and Art Nouveau*, ed. R. Koch, New York, 1970

    Exhibition of the l'Art Nouveau, Grafton Galleries, London, 1899

    Salon de l'Art Nouveau Catalogue, Paris, 1895

Bouilhet, André. "L'Exposition de Chicago," *Revue des Arts Décoratifs*, 14 (1893), 65–79

Breck, Joseph. "Louis C. Tiffany Window," *Metropolitan Museum of Art Bulletin*, 20 (1925), 287–88

Caffin, Charles H. "Decorated Windows," *The Craftsman*, III (March 1903), 356

Character and Individuality in Decorations and Furnishings, Tiffany Studios, 1913

Cole, Charles. "Painted Glass in Household Decoration," *Harper's Monthly*, LIX (October 1879), 655–64

Coleman, Caryl. "A Sea of Glass," *Architectural Record*, II (1893), 264–85

    "The Second Spring," *Architectural Record*, II (1893), 473–92

"A Comparative Study of European and American Church Glass," *House Beautiful* (April 1898), 143–48

Cook, Clarence. "Recent Church Decoration," *Scribner's Magazine* (February 1878), 569–77

De Cuers, René. "Domestic Stained Glass in France," *Architectural Record*, IX (1899), 115–41

Dekay, C. *The Art Work of Louis Comfort Tiffany*, New York, 1914

De Quelin, René. "This Te Deum Is Sung in Glass," *International Studio*, LXVI (1923), 360–61

Dreiser, Theodore. "The Making of Stained Glass Windows," *Cosmopolitan*, 26 (1899), 243–52

A Few Suggestions of Its Work (booklet), Tiffany Studios Ecclesiastical Department, 1911

Fox, Dorothea M. "Tiffany Glass," *Antiques*, XLIV (1943), 240–41, 295–96

Fred, A. W. "Interieurs von L. C. Tiffany," *Dekorative Kunst*, 9 (1901), 110–16

Fuchs, George. "Eindrücke aus der amerikanischen Abteilung," *Deutsche Kunst und Dekoration* (1902), 182–92

Gensel, W. "Tiffany-Gläser auf der Pariser Welt Ausstellung 1900," *Deutsche Kunst und Dekoration* (1900–01), 44–45, 86–93, 95–97

Glass Mosaics, Tiffany Glass and Decorating Company, 1896

Goodhue, Harry Eldredge. "Stained Glass in Private Houses," *Architectural Record*, XVIII (1905), 347–54

Harrison, Constance C. "Some Work of the Associated Artists," *Harper's Monthly*, LXIX (1884), 343–51

Holiday, Henry. *Stained Glass as an Art,* London, 1896
"How the Rich are Buried," *Architectural Record,* X (1900), 23–51
Howe, Samuel. "American Country House of Louis C. Tiffany," *International Studio,* XXXIII (February 1908), 294–96

Kaufmann, Edgar. "At Home with Louis C. Tiffany," *Interiors* (December 1957), 118–25, 183
    "Tiffany, Then and Now," *Interiors* (February 1955), 82–85
Kellogg, Cynthia. "Designs by Mr. Tiffany," *The New York Times Magazine,* 26 January 1958, 50–51
Koch, Robert. *Louis C. Tiffany: Rebel in Glass,* New York, 1964, 1966
    "Tiffany's Abstractions in Glass," *Antiques,* CV (June 1974), 1290–94

"L. C. Tiffany," *Dekorative Kunst,* 3 (1899), 108–20
La Cossitt, Henry. "Treasure House on Fifth Avenue," *The Saturday Evening Post,* 24 January 1953, 30–31, 102–06; 31 January 1953, 30, 108–11
A List of Windows, Tiffany Glass and Decorating Company, 1897
Lloyd, John Gilbert. *Stained Glass in America,* Jenkintown, Pa., 1963, p. 56
"The Long Island Home of Mr. Louis C. Tiffany," *Town and Country,* 6 September 1913, 24–26, 42
"Louis C. Tiffany," *Art Digest,* 1 February 1933
Low, Will H. "Old Glass in New Windows," *Scribner's Magazine* (1888), 675–86
Lyman, Clara Brown. "Recent Achievements in Decorative Lighting," *Country Life in America* (October 1914), 52–54

"A Many-sided Creator of the Beautiful," *Arts and Decoration,* 17 (1922), 176–77
Mausoleums, Tiffany Studios, 1914
Meier-Graefe, J. "M. Louis C. Tiffany," *L'Art Décoratif,* 1 (April 1898), 105, 106, 116–28
Memorial Tablets; Ancient and Modern, Tiffany Glass and Decorating Company, 1896
Memorial Windows, Tiffany Favrile Glass, Tablets, Mosaics, Tiffany Studios, 1897
Memorials in Glass and Stone, Tiffany Studios, 1913 (two editions)
The Mosaic Curtain for the National Theatre of Mexico, Tiffany Studios, 1911
"Mr. Louis C. Tiffany, Famous Artist in Stained Glass," *New York Herald Magazine,* 23 April 1916
"Mr. Louis C. Tiffany, Laurelton Hall at Cold Spring, Long Island," *The Spur,* 15 August 1914, 25–29

"On the Exhibit of Stained Glass at the Fair," *American Architect and Building News,* 11 November 1893, 74–75
Oppenheimer, Herbert. *Louis C. Tiffany: His Legacy,* Columbia University thesis (unpublished), New York, 1954

"The Painted Window," *The Craftsman,* III (March 1903), 348
A Partial List of Windows, Tiffany Studios, *c.* 1910
"Portrait of Louis C. Tiffany," *Arts and Decoration,* December 1921

"Revival of the Fanciest: Tiffany Glass," *Harper's Magazine,* September 1956, 80

Riordan, Roger. "American Stained Glass," *The American Art Review*, v. II
  (1881), Division 1, no. 18, 229–34; Division 2, no. 19, 7–11; no. 20, 59–64

Saks, Judith. "Tiffany's Household Decoration – A Landscape Window," *The
  Bulletin of the Cleveland Museum of Art*, October 1976, 227–35
Saylor, Henry H. "The Country Home of Mr. Louis C. Tiffany," *Country Life
  in America* (December 1908), 157–62
Schaefer, Herwin. "Tiffany's Fame in Europe," *The Art Bulletin*, 44 (December
  1962), 309–28
Sherwood, Stephen. *The Art of Frank Brangwyn*, London, 1924
Smith, Minna C. "Louis C. Tiffany – The Celestial Hierarchy," *International
  Studio*, XXXIII (February 1908), 96–99
Speenburg, Gertrude. *The Arts of the Tiffanys*, Chicago, 1956
Syford, E. *Examples of Recent Work from the Studios of Louis C. Tiffany*, Boston,
  1911
A Synopsis of the Exhibition at the World's Fair, Chicago, 1893, Tiffany Glass and
  Decorating Company, 1893

Thomas, William H. "Window Making as an Art," *Munsey's Magazine*, XXVI
  (December 1901), 386–95
Tiffany Favrile Glass Considered in Its Chronological Relationship, Tiffany Glass and
  Decorating Company, n.d.
"Tiffany Glass Reappraised," *Art in America*, 45, no. 4 (Winter 1957–58), 32
Tiffany, Louis C. "American Art Supreme in Colored Glass," *The Forum*, 15,
  no. 2 (1893), 621–28
  "American Progress in the Manufacture of Stained Glass," *Scribner's
Magazine* (1891), 485–86
  "Color and Its Kinship to Sound," *The Art World*, 2 (1917), 142–43
  The Dream Garden (booklet on the Curtis Publishing Co. mosaic),
Philadelphia
  "The Gospel of Good Taste," *Country Life in America* (November 1910), 105
  "The Quest of Beauty," *Harper's Bazaar* (December 1917), 43–44
  "The Tasteful Use of Light and Color in Artificial Illumination," *Scientific
American*, 104 (15 April 1911), 373
  "What Is the Quest for Beauty," *International Studio*, LVIII (1916), lxiii
"Tiffany Retrospective at the Museum of Contemporary Craft," *Craft
  Horizon*, 18 (March 1958), 40–41
"Tiffany's Great Curtain," *Art Digest* (15 October 1934)
"Tiffany's Home," *Architectural Record*, X (October 1900), 191–202
Townsend, Horace. "American and French Applied Art at the Grafton
  Galleries," *International Studio*, VIII (1899), 39–46
"A Tribute to Mr. Louis C. Tiffany," *Bulletin of the Stained Glass Association of
  America*, December 1928, 8–12

Van Tassel, Valentin. "Louis Comfort Tiffany," *The Antiques Journal*, v. 7
  (1952), no. 7, 19–21; no. 8, 13–15, 42

Waern, Cecilia. "The Industrial Arts of America, The Tiffany Glass &
  Decorating Company," *International Studio*, II (1897), 156–65; V (1898), 16–21

Weinberg, Barbara Helene. "The Early Stained Glass Work of John La Farge (1835–1910)," *Stained Glass,* LXVI (Summer 1972), 4–16

"John La Farge and the Invention of American Opalescent Windows," *Stained Glass,* LXVII (Autumn 1972), 4–11

Weir, Hugh. "Through the Looking Glass – An Interview with Louis Comfort Tiffany, *Collier's,* 23 May 1925

Weissberger, Herbert. "After Many Years: Tiffany Glass," *Carnegie Magazine,* 30 (October 1956), 256–68, 279

"The Window Opening in Decoration," *International Studio,* XXVI (1905), xvii

Appendix: A Partial list of Tiffany windows

The following list combines and updates the three which Tiffany Studios published in 1893 (as an Addendum to the Chicago Exposition booklet), 1897, and 1910. Strangely, the last one, entitled *A Partial List of Windows*, did not include all of those listed in the preceding two. These have been added here, in addition to later commissions which the author has researched. Extensive as the final list now is, it is still incomplete. No reference is made to Tiffany's domestic commissions or to most of the religious and institutional windows undertaken between 1910 and the firm's closure in 1932.

The scheme of the Tiffany Studios' 1910 list has been retained here. The five New York City boroughs were listed first, because of the relatively large number of commissions carried out there. The remaining windows in New York State come next, followed by commissions for the rest of the United States, listed alphabetically by State and town. The end of the list includes commissions from Canada and overseas.

The list is intended as a guide for the Tiffany enthusiast who wishes to view the windows *in situ*. One should bear in mind that a large number of churches and synagogues have changed their names over the last seventy years. It is best to consult the "Yellow Pages" for a town or area before setting out to visit a specific church. The "First Congregational Church" of 1910, for example, has by now almost certainly changed its name. Churches are listed by denomination in the "Yellow Pages," so the section on Congregational Churches will provide the present names of all which exist in a particular town. A telephone call to the church secretary will quickly identify whether that is the one for which one is looking. Bear in mind, in this respect, that church offices are often open only until noon from Monday to Friday and in summer sometimes not at all! Weekend viewing can also be difficult. Churches are frequently locked both on Saturdays and between services on Sundays. One should telephone for an appointment.

CHURCH OF THE ASCENSION,
EPISCOPAL, Fifth Ave. and 10th Street.
*The Rhinelander Memorial Window, "The
Resurrection."*
CHURCH OF THE COVENANT, 35th
Street and Park Avenue.
CHURCH OF THE INCARNATION,
EPISCOPAL, Madison Ave. and 35th Street.
The Hale Memorial Window, "The Pilgrim."
*The Britton Memorial Window, "Joseph
teaching Christ to be a Carpenter."*
*The Coles Memorial Window, "Raising of
Lazarus."*
*The Watson Memorial Window, "The Lord is
my Shepherd."*
Brooks Memorial Tablet.
Norwood Memorial Door.
CHURCH OF THE HEAVENLY REST,
EPISCOPAL, Fifth Ave. and 45th Street.
*The Howland Memorial Window, "Christ and
the Four Evangelists."*
TRINITY CHAPEL, EPISCOPAL, 25th
Street and Broadway.
Chancel Decorations.
ST. LUKE'S EPISCOPAL CHURCH, 10th
Ave. and 141st Street.
Ornamental Glass throughout Church.
ST. MICHAEL'S EPISCOPAL CHURCH,
Amsterdam Ave. and 99th Street.
*Chancel Window, "St. Michael and All
Angels."*
Chancel Decorations, Altar and Altar Rail.
ST. ANDREW'S EPISCOPAL CHURCH,
Fifth Ave. and 127th Street.
*Molloy Memorial Window, "Star of
Bethlehem."*
Bailey Memorial Window, "Angel of Faith."
ST. THOMAS EPISCOPAL CHURCH, Fifth
Avenue and 53rd Street.
*Woodward Memorial Window, "Dorcas and St.
Martin."*
*Schmelzel Memorial Window, "Jesus and the
Pilgrims."*
ALL ANGELS' EPISCOPAL CHURCH,
West End Avenue and 81st St (demolished
1978, windows sold at auction).
*Hoffman Memorial Window, "Blessed are the
pure in heart."*
Memorial Altar Cross.
*Memorial Windows, "Nativity," "Presentation
in Temple," "Condemnation," "Crucifixion,"
"Resurrection," "Ascension," "Creation,"
"Judgment," "Eight Beatitudes," "Benedicte."*
*Wicker Memorial Window, "Adoration of
Incarnation."*
CHRIST EPISCOPAL CHURCH, Boulevard
and 71st Street (now Bible Deliverance
Evangelistic Temple).
*Wilmerding Memorial Window, "St. John the
Baptist."*
Bell Memorial Window, "Madonna."
*Wallen Memorial Window, "Disputation in the
Temple."*
*Peck Memorial Window, "St. John the
Evangelist."*
*Hatch Memorial Window, "Christ Blessing
Little Children."*
Hadley Memorial Window, "St. Elizabeth."

CHURCH OF ZION AND ST. TIMOTHY,
EPISCOPAL, 57th Street and Seventh
Avenue.
Ornamental Windows.
ST. AGNES EPISCOPAL CHURCH, 92nd
Street and Ninth Avenue.
Chancel Decorations, Marble Mosaic Inlays.
Altar Hangings.
Ornamental Windows.
*Memorial Windows, "Noah and Abraham,"
"Doctors of the Western Church."*
HOLY TRINITY EPISCOPAL CHURCH,
Lenox Avenue and 122nd Street.
Ornamental Windows.
ST. JAMES EPISCOPAL CHURCH, Madison
Avenue and 71st Street.
*Smithers Memorial Window, "And in the morn
those Angel faces smile."*
War Memorial Window, "Angel of Praise."
CALVARY CHURCH, EPISCOPAL, Fourth
Avenue and 21st Street.
Mosaic Fountain.
CHURCH OF THE HOLY CROSS,
ROMAN CATHOLIC, 355 West 42nd
Street.
Ornamental Windows.
MIDDLE DUTCH CHURCH, REFORMED,
Second Avenue and 7th Street (now:
Collegiate Reformed Dutch Church).
*Ornamental Glass for Skylight, Sunday School,
front of Church.*
*West Window, "Arms of Reformed Church in
America."*
"Seal of Corporation."
"Floral Symbols."
*Side windows, illustrating scenes in the life of
Christ:*
Brower Memorial Window, "Visit of the Magi."
*Greenwood and Rudd Memorial Window,
"Jesus at Bethany."*
*Van Arsdal Memorial Window, "Christ
Blessing Little Children."*
*Brownlee Memorial Window, "Resurrection
Angel," "Boy Christ."*
*Louisa Chambers' Memorial Window, "Christ in
the Temple."*
*Chambers' Memorial Window, "Jesus and the
Woman of Samaria."*
*Hyde Memorial Window, "Glory to God in the
Highest."*
Cuyler & Jessup Memorial Windows.
COLLEGIATE REFORMED CHURCH,
West End Avenue and 77th Street.
*Jeremiah Memorial Window, "Lo! I stand at the
door and knock."*
SOUTH REFORMED CHURCH, Madison
Avenue and 38th Street.
*Memorial Window, "The Resurrection,"
"Adoration of the Kings."*
CHURCH OF THE SACRED HEART,
ROMAN CATHOLIC, 477 West 51st
Street.
Ornamental Windows.
ST. FRANCIS XAVIER'S SCHOOL
CHAPEL, ROMAN CATHOLIC, 16th
Street and Sixth Avenue.
Ornamental Windows.
ST. MICHAEL'S ROMAN CATHOLIC
CHURCH, Ninth Avenue and 32nd Street.
Tablets under windows.
ST. JAMES LUTHERAN CHURCH, Madison

Avenue and 73rd Street.
*Unangst Memorial, "Christ and Mary and
Martha."*
Von Post Memorial, "Christ in Glory."
*Kerfoot Memorial Window, "Star of
Bethlehem."*
CHRIST LUTHERAN CHURCH, 406 East
19th Street.
Chancel Windows, Ornamental.
ST. JAMES ROMAN CATHOLIC CHURCH,
James Street.
Two Window, Floral Design.
Altar, Decorations.
ST. BERNARD'S ROMAN CATHOLIC
CHURCH, 14th Street and 8th Avenue.
Ornamental Windows.
Chancel Windows, "The Crucifixion."
*Transept Windows, "The Nativity," "The
Resurrection."*
ST. GABRIEL'S ROMAN CATHOLIC
CHURCH, 37th Street and Second Avenue.
Transept Window, "The Ascension."
Ornamental Windows.
ST. IGNATIUS LOYOLA, ROMAN
CATHOLIC CHURCH, Park Avenue and
84th Street.
Ornamental Glass for Baptistry Dome.
ALL SOULS' CHURCH, UNITARIAN,
Fourth Avenue and 20th Street.
Dome Glass, Ornamental.
TEMPLE SHAARAY TEFILA, West End
Avenue and 82nd Street.
Decorations.
TEMPLE SHEARITH ISRAEL, Central Park
West and 70th Street (now: Congregation
Shearith Israel).
Ornamental Windows.
Decorations.
FOURTH PRESBYTERIAN CHURCH,
W. 104th St.
*Marshall Memorial Window, "The
Transfiguration."*
Marshall Memorial Window, "Ascension."
CHAPEL OF THE ASSOCIATION OF THE
HOME FOR THE RELIEF OF
RESPECTABLE AGED AND INDIGENT
FEMALES.
Nixon Memorial Window, Ornamental.
McCorkle Memorial Window, Ornamental.
Dunning Memorial Window, Ornamental.
Innis Memorial Window, Ornamental.
Minton Memorial Window Ornamental.
(Both of the above were burnt down in the
1977 blackout).
PRESBYTERIAN CHURCH (High Bridge).
Rose Window, Ornamental.
Ornamental Windows.
PRESBYTERIAN CHURCH, Fifth Ave. and
11th St.
McJimsey Memorial Window, "Isaiah."
Moir Memorial Window, "Columba."
OLIVET CHAPEL, PRESBYTERIAN,
Second Avenue and Second Street.
Ornamental Windows.
FIFTH AVENUE PRESBYTERIAN
CHURCH, Fifth Avenue and 55th Street.
Decorations.
CALVARY BAPTIST CHURCH, 57th St.
and 7th Ave.
*Cauldwell Memorial Window, "Christ
Blessing Little Children."*

MADISON AVENUE BAPTIST CHURCH,
Madison Avenue and 31st Street.
Decorations.
BAPTIST CHURCH OF EPIPHANY,
Madison Ave. and 64th St.
Leask Memorial Window, "Christ Walking on Water."
Lesher Memorial Window, "Baptism."
Conklin Memorial Window, "Leading to Christ."
Hamlin Memorial Window, Ornamental.
Henop Memorial Window, Ornamental.
McKim Memorial Window, Ornamental.
CHURCH OF THE ADVENT.
Kaltenbach Memorial Window, "St. Paul Preaching at Athens."
Groh Memorial Window, "Advent."
Zollikoffer Memorial Windows, Ornamental Windows.
Greenwood Memorial Window, "Christ Blessing Children."
CHURCH OF HOLY INNOCENCE, 37th
Street and Broadway.
Ornamental Windows.
FIFTH AVENUE BAPTIST CHURCH.
Cobby Memorial Window, "Baptism."
HOLY TRINITY EVANGELICAL
LUTHERAN CHURCH, 65th St. and
Central Park West.
Hunter Memorial Window, "Second Advent."
LENOX AVENUE UNITARIAN CHURCH,
Lenox Avenue and 121st Street.
Jackson Memorial Window, Ornamental.
ST. LEO'S ROMAN CATHOLIC CHURCH.
Raborg Memorial Window.
ST. PATRICK'S CATHEDRAL.
Ornamental Window.
ST. FRANCIS XAVIER ROMAN CATHOLIC
CHURCH, 16th St. and 6th Ave.
Copenhagen Memorial Window, "Madonna and Child."
Stanton Memorial Window, "Angel of Resurrection."
Taylor Memorial Window, "Faith, Hope and Charity."
Warren Memorial Window, Ornamental.
Smithers Memorial Window, Ornamental.
Memorial Window, "Lord Who Shall Abide in Thy Tabernacle."
ST. PETER'S EPISCOPAL CHURCH,
20th St. and 9th Ave.
Wiswall Memorial Window, "Easter Morn."
Kidder Memorial Window, "Return of the Soul."
Howell Memorial Window, "Valiant Woman."
Gorman Memorial Window, "Woman of Samaria."
Livingston Memorial Window.
Wilcoxson Memorial, "Christ Blessing Children."
Douglas Memorial.
Roche Memorial.
Faber Memorial.
TEMPLE EMMANUEL, 65th St. and 5th Ave.
Memorial Window, Landscape.
MADISON AVENUE PRESBYTERIAN
CHURCH.
Johnson Memorial Window, "Angels."
Williams Memorial Window, "Cross, Crown and Lilies."
Ornamental Windows.
MADISON SQUARE PRESBYTERIAN
CHURCH.
Medallion Windows.
MARBLE COLLEGIATE CHURCH, Fifth
Ave. and 29th Street.
Dayton Memorial Window, "Moses in the Burning Bush."
Sandham Memorial Window, "Joshua."
METROPOLITAN TEMPLE.
Lincoln Memorial Window, "Equal Liberty to All."
Roosevelt Memorial Window, "Equal Justice to All."
Marble and Glass Mosaic Pulpit and Decorations.
NEW PRESBYTERIAN CHURCH,

Brainbridge Ave. and Southern Boulevard.
London Memorial Window, Ornamental.
AMITY BAPTIST CHURCH, 54th St. and
8th Ave.
Wilson Etched Bronze Tablet.
ST. NICHOLAS CHURCH, 48th St. and 5th
Ave.
Runk, Two Carved Hyman Boards.
CHURCH OF THE PURITAN, 130th St.
and 5th Ave.
Spaulding Bronze Tablet and Carved Frame.
ST. PAUL'S SCHOOL, Church and Vesey
Streets.
Ornamental Glass.
GENERAL THEOLOGICAL SEMINARY,
Chelsea Square.
Ornamental Windows in Deanery.
ACADEMY OF THE SACRED HEART,
533 Madison Avenue.
Chapel Windows, "Angels."
COLUMBIA COLLEGE LIBRARY, Madison
Avenue and 50th Street.
Class Window, 'Socrates."
Class Window, "Virgil."
NORMAL COLLEGE, 68th St. and Park
Avenue.
Neustadt Memorial Window.
Class of '97 Window, Ornamental.
Class of '98, Ornamental.
BERKELEY SCHOOL, 44th Street and Fifth
Avenue (destroyed).
Billings Memorial Window, "Plato Teaching Aristotle."
White Memorial Window, Ornamental.
Franklin Memorial Window, "The Young Alexander."
Reynal Memorial Window, "David, the Armor-Bearer of Saul."
Granberry Memorial Window, "Youth and the Four Elements."
Fuller Memorial Window, "The Youthful Joseph."
UNIVERSITY HEIGHTS, NEW YORK
UNIVERSITY.
Memorial Window, "Vertitas."
Ornamental Skylights.
NEW YORK PUBLIC LIBRARY, 42nd St.
and 5th Ave.
Williams Etched Bronze Tablet.
SEVENTH REGIMENT ARMORY, Park
Avenue and 67th Street.
Decorations in Veterans Room, etc.
ORTHOPAEDIC HOSPITAL, 126 East 59th
Street.
Gracie Memorial Window, Ornamental.
NURSERY AND CHILD'S HOSPITAL,
Lexington Avenue and 49th Street.
Floyd Memorial Window, "Lilies and Crown."
POST GRADUATE HOSPITAL, Second Ave.
and 20th Street.
Thompson Memorial Window, "Recreation and Music" (window removed).
NEW YORK HOSPITAL, 15th Street.
Ornamental Windows.
HUDSON THEATRE, 45th Street and
Broadway (demolished).
Ornamental Windows.
STUYVESANT THEATRE (demolished).
Ornamental Window.
LYCEUM THEATRE, Fourth Avenue and
23rd Street (demolished 1902).
Decorations.
SAVOY HOTEL, Fifth Avenue and 59th
Street (demolished).
Ornamental Windows.
Decorations, Furniture and Hangings.
WALDORF ASTORIA.
Ornamental Windows.
MANHATTAN HOTEL, Madison Avenue and
42nd Street.
Marble and Glass Mosaic Inlays.
ANSONIA APARTMENTS, 1730 Broadway.
Ornamental Windows.
METROPOLITAN LIFE INSURANCE
BUILDING, 23rd St. and Madison Ave.
Ornamental Dome.
NEW YORK CLEARING HOUSE.
Ornamental Windows.

COTTON EXCHANGE, Broad Street.
Ornamental Window.
NEW YORK LIFE BUILDING.
Ornamental Windows.
R. G. DUN BUILDING, 290 Broadway.
Ornamental Skylight.
JOHNSON BUILDING, Exchange Place.
Ornamental Windows.
RAQUET AND TENNIS CLUB, 43rd Street.
Ornamental Windows.
AUTOMOBILE CLUB OF AMERICA, 58th
St. and 5th Ave.
Ornamental Windows.
COLONIAL CLUB, Boulevard and 72nd
Street (demolished).
Stairway Window, "Van Corlears, the Trumpeter."
PLAYERS CLUB, Gramercy Park.
Reading-room Windows, Ornamental.
UNION LEAGUE CLUB, Fifth Avenue and
39th Street.
Decorations, Main Hall.
Large Staircase Windows.
LAWYER'S CLUB, Equitable Building.
Ornamental Colored Windows.
DOWN TOWN CLUB, 60 Pine Street.
Large Stairway Window.
UNIVERSITY CLUB, Madison Avenue and
26th Street.
HOBOKEN LINE: Ferry boats "Bremen," "Hamburg," "Secaucus," and "Bergen."

Brooklyn
ST. GEORGE'S EPISCOPAL CHURCH,
Marcy, corner Gates Avenue.
Sayres Memorial Window, "Our Saviour."
Glover Memorial Window, "Christ in the Temple."
ST. LUKE'S EPISCOPAL CHURCH, Clinton
Avenue and Fulton Street (now: St. Luke
and St. Matthew).
Annan Memorial Window, "Christ and the Woman of Samaria."
Gardner Memorial Window, "Star of Bethlehem."
Gardner Memorial Window, "Adoration of the Magi."
GRACE EPISCOPAL CHURCH, Grace Court
and Hicks Street.
Husted Memorial Window, "Our Saviour, and the Symbols of the Evangelists."
Litchfield Memorial Window, "Adoration of the Madonna."
ST. MARY'S EPISCOPAL CHURCH,
Classon Avenue.
Johnson Memorial Window, "Feed my Lambs."
ST. ANN'S EPISCOPAL CHURCH,
Clinton Street.
DeWitt Memorial Window, "The Good Shepherd."
CHURCH OF THE HOLY TRINITY,
EPISCOPAL, Montague Street (now: St.
Ann and the Holy Trinity).
Elliott Memorial Window, "St. Peter."
CHRIST EPISCOPAL CHURCH, Bedford
Avenue and Morton Street.
Bearns Memorial Window, "Christ Blessing Little Children."
ST. CATHERINE ROMAN CATHOLIC
CHURCH, Bushwick Avenue corner Ten
Eyck Street.
Lyons Memorial Window, "Chalice, Vine and Passion Flowers."
CHURCH OF THE TRANSFIGURATION,
ROMAN CATHOLIC, Marcy Avenue and
Hooper Street.
Gable and Porch Lights.
Windows for Church, "Four Evangelists."
"St. Agnes."
"St. Cecilia."
"St. Mary Magdalene."
"Madonna and Child."
"St. Dominic."
"St. Peter and Paul."
Ornamental Windows.
SOUTH CONGREGATIONAL CHURCH,
Fourth Place and Court Street.
Ornamental Windows.

CONVENT OF MERCY, Classon and
Willoughby Avenues.
Ornamental Windows.
Decorations.
FIRST PRESBYTERIAN CHURCH, Henry
and Clark Streets.
Stewart Memorial Window, "Guardian Angel."
*Sheldon Memorial Window, "Christ and the
Fishermen."*
Ornamental Glass, Dome Light over Pulpit.
Smith Memorial Window, "St. John."
Hine Memorial Window, "Angel of Victory."
*Babcock Memorial Window, "Christ at House of
Mary and Martha."*
SOUTH THIRD STREET PRESBYTERIAN
CHURCH, South Third Street and Driggs
Avenue (rebuilt in 1968).
*Joseph Arthur Burr Memorial Window
Ornamental.*
*Seeley and Alstine Memorial Windows,
Ornamental.*
Cole Memorial Window, Ornamental.
Wells Memorial Window, Ornamental.
Howell Memorial Window, Ornamental.
Ornamental Windows.
LAFAYETTE AVENUE PRESBYTERIAN
CHURCH, Lafayette Avenue corner S.
Oxford Street.
*Pease Memorial Window, "Christ in the
Temple."*
Fahys Memorial Window, "The Nativity."
Gregg Memorial Window, "Baptism of Christ."
*Palmer Memorial Window, "Christ Blessing
Little Children."*
*Cuyler Memorial Window, "St. Paul Preaching
at Athens."*
MEMORIAL PRESBYTERIAN CHURCH,
St. John's Place and Seventh Avenue.
*Woodford Memorial Window, "St. Elizabeth of
Hungary."*
*Robertson Memorial Window, "Parable of the
Talents."*
*Bayliss Memorial Window, "Christ Blessing
Little Children."*
*Bryan Memorial Window, "Angel of Mercy"
and "St. Agnes."*
Memorial Window, "Three Marys at Tomb."
Pearson Memorial Window, "Good Shepherd."
PRESBYTERIAN CHURCH, 81st Street and
Second Avenue (Bay Ridge).
Rose Window, "Our Saviour."
ST. MATTHEW'S LUTHERAN CHURCH,
Sixth Avenue and Second Street.
*Schieren Memorial Window, "Cross and
Cherubs Heads."*
CHURCH OF THE UNITY, Gates Avenue,
corner Irving Place.
Memorial Window, Ornamental.
Foster Memorial Window, Ornamental.
Memorial Window, Ornamental.
CHURCH OF THE SAVIOUR, Pierrepont
Street and Monroe Place (now: First
Unitarian Church).
Memorial Window, "Our Saviour."
*Low Memorial Window, "Workers in the
Vineyard."*
*Woodward Memorial Window, "Christ
Blessing Little Children."*
Frothingham Memorial Window, "David."
Farley Memorial Window, "The Sower."
WASHINGTON AVENUE BAPTIST
CHURCH, Washington, corner Gates
Avenue (now: Brown Memorial Baptist
Church).
Bedford Memorial Window, Ornamental.
Patton Memorial Window, Ornamental.
Cotton Memorial Window, Ornamental.
Harding Memorial Window, Symbolical.
Dingee Memorial Window, "The Pilgrims."
Dingee Memorial Window, "The Resurrection."
Ornamental Windows.
FIRST REFORMED DUTCH CHURCH,
Seventh Avenue and Carroll Street.
*Cortelyou Memorial Window, "Parable of the
Talents."*
*Kissam Memorial Window, "Christ and the
woman of Samaria."*
REFORMED CHURCH OF THE HEIGHTS,

Pierrepont Street, near Monroe Place.
*Bethune Memorial Window, "Light of the
World."*
*Memorial Window, "Child Christ in the
Temple."*
Memorial Window, Ornamental.
Ornamental Windows.
CHURCH OF THE PILGRIMS, Henry and
Remsen Streets.
*Chittenden Memorial Window, "Scenes in the
Life of Christ."*
*Thayer Memorial Window, "Cornelius and the
Angel."*
CALVARY BAPTIST CHURCH.
Ornamental.
CHURCH OF TRANSFIGURATION.
*Windows for Church, "St. Augustine," "St.
Patrick," "St. Denis of France." "St. Boniface,"
and "St. John the Baptist."*
NEW JERUSALEM CHURCH, Monroe
Place and Clark Street.
*Journeay Memorial Window, "Archangel
Raphael."*
BEECHER MEMORIAL CHURCH.
Bailey Memorial Window, Ornamental.
CHRIST EPISCOPAL CHURCH (Clinton
and Harrison Streets).
*Orr Memorial Windows, "Resurrection Morn"
and "Confession of Faith."*
*Thomas Memorial Window, "Raising of
Lazarus."*
*Van Brunt Memorial Window, "Christ in
Temple."*
CHURCH OF CHRIST SCIENTIST.
Ornamental Windows.
CHURCH OF MESSIAH (demolished).
Baker Memorial Window, "Christ Child."
Cole Memorial Window, "St. Peter and John."
*Loundsbury Memorial Window, "Christ
Blessing Children."*
*Van Nostrand Memorial Window, "Angel with
Lilies."*
Wallace Memorial Window, "Return of Soul."
*Stillman Memorial Window, "Valiant
Woman."*
*Chapman Memorial Window, "St. Augustine
and St. Monica."*
*Hollingshead Memorial Windows, "Angels of
Praise" and Landscape.*
*Mason Memorial Window, "Presentation in
Temple."*
CLASSON AVENUE PRESBYTERIAN
CHURCH (Classon Avenue and Monroe
Street).
*Anderson Memorial Window, "St. Paul
Preaching at Athens."*
CLINTON AVE. CONGREGATIONAL
CHURCH.
Olyphant Memorial Window, "Charity."
EAST NEW YORK REFORMED CHURCH.
Brooks Memorial Window.
HANSOM PLACE METHODIST EPIS.
CHURCH.
*French Memorial Window, "Christ Blessing
Children."*
*Strout Memorial Window, "Christ and Rich
Young Man."*
LEE AVENUE CONGREGATIONAL
CHURCH.
Ornamental Windows.
LEE AVENUE PRESBYTERIAN CHURCH.
Ornamental Windows.
NEW UTRECHT REFORMED CHURCH.
*Van Brunt Memorial Window, "Lord is My
Shepherd."*
EPISCOPAL CHURCH OF
RECONCILIATION.
Ornamental Windows.
ST. AUGUSTINE'S CHURCH.
Ornamental Windows.
ST. GEORGE'S PROTESTANT EPIS.
CHURCH.
*Glover Memorial Window, "Christ in the
Temple."*
ST. JAMES EPISCOPAL CHURCH.
DeWitt Memorial Window, "Angel."
ST. LUKE'S GERMAN LUTHERAN
CHURCH.

*Friedhoff Memorial Window, "Light of the
World."*
*Manheim Memorial Window, "Christ
Appearing to Mary."*
*Hadley Memorial Window, "Gabriel and
Raphael."*
SANDS STREET CHURCH.
Barnier Memorial Window, "Come Unto Me."
TRINITY EVANGELICAL CHURCH
(Lutheran Cemetery).
Hunter Memorial Window, "Holy Trinity."
TEMPLE ISRAEL.
Ornamental Window.
PRATT INSTITUTE.
Ornamental Windows.
Decorations.
PACKER INSTITUTE.
*Backus Memorial Window, "Dante, Virgil and
Beatrice."*
*Carpenter Memorial Window, "Science and
Literature."*
Caruana Memorial Window, "Education."
*King Memorial Window, "My Soul Illuminates
Me."*
Memorial Window, "Hope."
HOME FOR THE AGED.
Taylor Memorial Window, Ornamental.
ST. GEORGE'S HOTEL, Clark Street.
Ornamental Window.
GIRLS HIGH SCHOOL.
*Lewis Memorial Window, "Alquin and
Charlemagne."*
ST. PAUL'S SCHOOL.
*Newcomb Memorial Window, "Conversion of
St. Paul."*
HOTEL TOURAINE.
Ornamental Windows.
ST. JOHN EPISCOPAL HOSPITAL, Albany
and Atlantic Avenues.
Chapel Window, Ornamental.

NEW YORK STATE
Adirondacks
EPISCOPAL CHURCH.
Bird Memorial Window, "Climbs."

Albany
ST. PETER'S EPISCOPAL CHURCH.
Memorial Window, Rose.
Ornamental Window.
ST. PAUL'S EPISCOPAL CHURCH.
Wilson Memorial Window, "Good Shepherd."
FIRST REFORMED CHURCH.
Sumner Memorial, Landscape, 1912.
FIRST PRESBYTERIAN CHURCH.
Meeting Memorial, Landscape.
Strong Memorial, Landscape.
MADISON AVENUE REFORMED
CHURCH (burnt down in 1937).
*Lansing Memorial Window, "Triumphant
Angels."*
Lansing, Decorations.
BETH EMETH SYNAGOGUE, Lancaster
Street.
Ornamental Windows.
Sporborg Memorial Window, "Moses."

Albion
MEMORIAL UNIVERSALIST CHURCH.
Ornamental Windows.
Memorial Window, "Christ the Consoler."

Amenia
ST. THOMAS EPISCOPAL CHURCH.
Memorial Window, "Hope."
Knibloe Memorial Window, "St. John."

Amsterdam
SECOND PRESBYTERIAN CHURCH.
*Gregory Memorial Window, "Vision of the
Angel from Revelations."*
Memorial Window, "The Ascension."
*Sanford Memorial Windows, "Paul Preaching at
Athens" and "Christ and Pilgrims."*

Angelica
ST. PAUL'S EPISCOPAL CHURCH.
Charles Memorial Window, "St. Luke."

Astoria, L. I.
CHURCH OF REDEEMER.
Lockwood Memorial Window, "Cornelius and Angel."

Auburn
WILLARD MEMORIAL CHAPEL.
Ornamental Windows.
Memorial Window, "Christ Walking on the Sea."
Chapel Decorations; Memorial Tablet; Furniture; Mosaic Floors.
CENTRAL PRESBYTERIAN CHURCH
(now: the Westminster Presbyterian Church).
Seward/Watson Memorial Window, Landscape.

Aurora
WELLS COLLEGE.
Isham Memorial Window, Ornamental.

Balston Spa
PRESBYTERIAN CHURCH.

Bath, Steuben Co.
NEW PRESBYTERIAN CHURCH.
Ornamental Windows.
Decorations.
Davenport Memorial Window, Ornamental.

Bay Ridge
PRESBYTERIAN CHURCH.
Dowling Memorial Window, "Figure of Christ."
DUTCH REFORMED CHURCH.
Van Brunt Memorial Window, "Resurrection."

Bayside, L. I.
ALL SAINTS' EPISCOPAL CHURCH.
Armstrong Memorial Window, "Angel of Resurrection."

Binghamton
FIRST PRESBYTERIAN CHURCH.
Ornamental Windows.
Decorations.

Briarcliff Manor
CONGREGATIONAL CHURCH.
Law Memorial Windows, Landscape, "Supper at Emmaus," "Nathaniel Before Christ."
Denman Memorial Window, "Christ Blessing Children."

Buffalo
FIRST PRESBYTERIAN CHURCH.
Ornamental Windows.
Mitchell Memorial Window, "Angel Faces."
Memorial Window, "St. Luke."
White Memorial Window, "Ascension."
TEMPLE BETH ZION (destroyed by fire, circa 1959).
Marcus Memorial Window, Ornamental.
Bergman Memorial Window, Ornamental.
Geirshofer Memorial Window, Ornamental.
Altman Memorial Window, Ornamental.
Warner Memorial Window, Ornamental.
Warner Memorial Window, Ornamental.
Warner Memorial Window, Ornamental.
TRINITY EPISCOPAL CHURCH.
Memorial Window, "The Annunciation."
Memorial Window, "Christ Making the Blind to See."
Memorial Window, "Christ and Matthew."
Memorial Window, "Gabriel and Raphael."
Memorial Window, "St. Cecilia."
FIRST CONGREGATIONAL CHURCH.
Ornamental Windows.
INGERSOLL MEMORIAL CHAPEL.
Memorial Window, "The Good Shepherd."
Matthews Memorial Window, "Purity."
Matthews Memorial Window, "St. Paul."
Rumsey Memorial Window.

ST. PAUL'S CHURCH.
Chancel Window.
Stevenson Memorial Window, "Flight of Angels."
ROMAN CATHOLIC CHURCH OF HOLY ANGELS.
Apinn Memorial Window, "Mary and Joseph."
WESTMINSTER CHURCH.
Ornamental Windows.
CHURCH OF THE GOOD SHEPHERD.
Ingersoll Memorial Window.

Cambridge
ST. LUKE'S CHURCH.
Wright Memorial Windows.
Wright Memorial Window, "John and Two Heads."

Campbell
FIRST PRESBYTERIAN CHURCH.
Clawson Memorial Window, Ornamental.

Catskill
ST. LUKE'S EPISCOPAL CHURCH.
Boyd Memorial Window, "Angel of Faith."

Centre Dunwoodie
SEMINARY CHAPEL.
Corrigan Memorial Window, "Our Lady."

Clyde
ST. JOHN'S EPISCOPAL CHURCH.
Memorial Window.

Cold Spring Harbor
ST. JOHN'S EPISCOPAL CHURCH.
Bleecker Memorial Window, "Angel of the Resurrection."
Jones-Bleecker Memorial Window, "Annunciation."
Jones Memorial Window, "Good Shepherd."

Cooperstown
PRESBYTERIAN CHURCH.
Phinney Memorial Window, Ornamental.
Beadle Memorial Window, Ornamental.
CHRIST CHURCH.
Dodge Memorial Window, "Charity."

Corning
CHRIST EPISCOPAL CHURCH.
Bigelow Memorial Window, "The Resurrection."
Ornamental Windows.
Hoare Memorial Window, "Cornelius and the Angel."
Tully Memorial Window, "Christ and Faith."

Danville
SANITORIUM CHAPEL.
Doctor Jackson Memorial Window, "Our Saviour."

Deposit
CHRIST CHURCH.
Van Schoyk Memorial Window, Ornamental.

Dickinson
BAPTIST CHURCH.
Ornamental Window.

East Chester
ST. JOHN'S CHURCH.
Pinckney Memorial Window, "Christ Walking on the Water."

Elizabethtown
CONGREGATIONAL CHURCH.
Hull Memorial Window, Ornamental.

Elmhurst, L. I.
PRESBYTERIAN CHURCH.
Leverich Memorial Window, "Founder of Church Ministering to Indians."

Elmira
TRINITY EPISCOPAL CHURCH.
Diven Memorial Window, "The Crusader."

FIRST PRESBYTERIAN CHURCH.
Gillett Memorial Window, "The Ascension."
PARK CONGREGATIONAL CHURCH.
Rapelyea, Two Marble Tablets.

Esopus
ASCENSION CHURCH.
Bookman Memorial Window, "Christ Blessing Children."

Far Rockaway
PRESBYTERIAN CHURCH (now: First Presbyterian Church).
Ornamental Windows.
SAGE MEMORIAL CHAPEL.
Sage Memorial Window, Landscape.

Fisher's Island
ST. JOHN'S EPISCOPAL CHURCH.
Memorial Window, "Our Saviour."

Fishkill Landing
ST. ANDREW'S EPISCOPAL CHURCH.
Rider Memorial Window, "Resurrection Angel."
Davies Memorial Window, "Good Shepherd."
Ornamental Windows.

Fishkill Village
LITTLE DUTCH CHURCH.
Brower Memorial Windows, "Resurrection Angel" and "Boy Christ."

Flatbush, L. I.
GRACE CHAPEL.
Lefferts Memorial Windows, "Angel of Victory," "Angel of Resurrection."
Longmeyer Memorial Window, "Hope."
DUTCH REFORMED CHURCH.
Lott Memorial Window, "St. John."
Hegeman Memorial Window, Ornamental.
Williamson Memorial Window, Ornamental.
Schoonmaker Memorial Window, Ornamental.
Ditmas Memorial Window, Ornamental.
Memorial Window, "Good Shepherd."
Garvin Memorial Window, Ornamental.
Prince Memorial Window, "Christ Blessing Little Children."
Vanderbilt Memorial Window, Ornamental.
Lefferts Memorial Window, Ornamental.
Martense Memorial Window, "Moses Striking the Rock."
Vanderveer Memorial Window, Ornamental.
Cortelyou Memorial Window, Ornamental.
Story Memorial Window, Ornamental.
Schenck Memorial Window, Ornamental.
Stryker Memorial Window, Ornamental.
Zabriski Memorial Window, "St. Luke."
Ornamental Windows.

Florida
PRESBYTERIAN CHURCH.
Pearson Memorial Window, Ornamental.

Flushing
REFORMED CHURCH.
Cobb Memorial Window.
Demarest Memorial Windows, "Easter Lilies."
Northrup Memorial Windows, "Floral and Ornamental."
ST. GEORGE'S EPISCOPAL CHURCH.
Memorial Window, for Sunday School Children.
Leggett Memorial Window, "Christ Healing Peter's Wife's Mother."

Fonda
DUTCH REFORMED CHURCH.
Hees Memorial Window, "Benediction."

Fordham
REFORMED MEMORIAL CHAPEL.
Ornamental Windows.
ST. JAMES EPISCOPAL CHURCH.
Schwab Memorial Window, "The Last Supper."
Holt Memorial Window, "Easter Morning."
Tiffany Memorial Window, "Lilies and Apple Blossoms."
Wheeler Memorial Window, Ornamental.

ST. JOHN'S COLLEGE.
Richards Memorial Windows, "Sacred Heart,"
"Virgin," "St. Joseph," "John the Evangelist,"
"St. Elizabeth of Hungary," "Blessed Margaret
Mary," Ornamental.

Fort Hamilton
ST. JOHN'S PROTESTANT EPISCOPAL
CHURCH.
Vanderpool Memorial Window, "Benediction."

Fort Wadsworth
ST. JOHN'S CHURCH.
Dans Memorial Window, "Cornelius and
Angel."

Garden City, L. I.
CHAPEL OF ST. PAUL'S SCHOOL.
Memorial Window, "Conversion of St. Paul."

Geneseo
ST. MICHAEL'S EPISCOPAL CHURCH.
Wadsworth Memorial Window, "Faith, Hope
and Charity."
PRESBYTERIAN CHURCH.

Geneva
NORTH PRESBYTERIAN CHURCH.
Hopkins Memorial Window, "Dorcas."
Camp Memorial Window, "Christ and the
Pilgrim."
McBLAIN MEMORIAL CHAPEL.
Fast Memorial Window, "Angel of
Resurrection," and Ornamenta.

Glen Cove
ST. PAUL'S EPISCOPAL CHURCH.
Russell Memorial Window.

Glen Falls
CHURCH OF THE MESSIAH, EPISCOPAL.
Pardo Memorial Window, "Our Saviour."
METHODIST EPISCOPAL CHURCH.
McEchran Memorial Window, "Christ Blessing
Children."
Roberts Memorial Window, Ornamental.
Little Memorial Window, Ornamental.

Great Neck
ALL SAINTS' EPISCOPAL CHURCH.
Hamilton Memorial Window, "Sermon on the
Mount."
Childs Memorial Window, "Angel of Praise."
Ornamental Windows.
Farnham Memorial Window, "Angel with
Landscape."
BAPTIST CHURCH.

Great River
EMMANUEL EPISCOPAL CHURCH.
Hobbs Memorial Window, "Christ and Child
with Adoring Angels," and Ornamental.

Haverstraw
CENTRAL PRESBYTERIAN CHURCH.
Fowler Memorial Window, "Ascension."
Babcock Memorial Window, Ornamental.
Bennett Memorial Window, Ornamental.
Bonsall Memorial Window, Ornamental.
Carr Memorial Window, Ornamental.
Cleary Memorial Window, Ornamental.
Cooper Memorial Window, Ornamental.
Freyfogle Memorial Window, Ornamental.
Hedges Memorial Window, Ornamental.
Oldfield Memorial Window, Ornamental.
Reynolds Memorial Window, Ornamental.
Freeman Memorial Window, "Road to
Emmaus."
TRINITY EPISCOPAL CHURCH.
West Memorial Window, "Angel of
Resurrection."

Hempstead
METHODIST CHURCH.
Thorne Memorial Window, "The Resurrection."

High Bridge
UNION REFORMED CHURCH.

Hollis
ST. GABRIEL'S PROTESTANT EPIS.
CHURCH.
Lott Memorial Window, Ornamental.

Hornell
CHRIST CHURCH.
Girls' Friendly Society, "Resurrection Angel."

Hornellsville
CHRIST EPISCOPAL CHURCH.
Windsor Memorial Window, "Good Shepherd."
ST. PAUL'S PROTESTANT EPISCOPAL
CHURCH.
Windsor Memorial Window, "St. Luke."
UNIVERSALIST CHURCH.
Greenbough Memorial Window, "Angel of
Peace and Mercy."

Horseheads
PRESBYTERIAN CHURCH.
Van Duzer Memorial Window, "Good
Shepherd."

Irvington
ST. BARNABAS EPISCOPAL CHURCH.
Baptistry Window, "The Holy Spirit."
Balcom Reredos in caen stone and marble.
Benjamin Memorial Window, Rose Window.

Islip
ST. MARK'S EPISCOPAL CHURCH.
Redmond Memorial Window, "St. John."
Carroll Memorial Window, "Choir of Angels."
Hyde Memorial Window, "Recording Angel."
Peters Memorial Window, Floral Design.

Ithaca
CORNELL UNIVERSITY.
Strong Memorial Window, Ornamental.
CONGREGATIONAL CHURCH.
Bush Memorial Window, "Figure of Christ."

Keene Valley
FELSENHEIM CHAPEL.
Lauring Memorial Window, "The Christian
Soldier."

Kenisco
KENISCO CEMETERY.
Berckman Mausoleum, Ornamental.
Kissam Mausoleum, Ornamental.
Moore Mausoleum, Landscape.
Reynolds Mausoleum, "Gethsemane."

Kingsbridge
CHURCH OF THE MEDIATOR.
Douglas Memorial Window, "Christ Blessing
Children."

Kingston
ST. JAMES METHODIST CHURCH.
Romer Memorial Window, "Angel of
Consolation."
FIRST REFORMED CHURCH.
Houghteling Memorial Window, "Presentation
in the Temple."

Lake Geneva
EPISCOPAL CHURCH.

Lake Kushaqua
MEM. HALL OF STONYWOLD
SANITORIUM.
Geer Memorial Window, "Good Shepherd and
Landscape."

Liberty
LOOMIS SANITORIUM.
Loomis Memorial Windows, "Faith," and
Ornamental.

Little Falls
FAIRVIEW CEMETERY.
Ingham Mausoleum, "Angels."

Lockport
FIRST PRESBYTERIAN CHURCH.
Arnold and Wisner Memorial Windows,
"Good Shepherd" and "Angels of Sight."
Ashley Memorial Window, "Resurrection."
Ferguson Memorial Window, "King David with
Angels."
Pomeroy Memorial Window, "I Am the Way,
the Truth and the Life."
Potter Memorial Window, "Christ Knocking at
the Door."
Gatskill Memorial Window.

Lyria
FIRST CONGREGATIONAL CHURCH.
Cadmus Memorial Window, "Nativity."

Manlius
CHRIST EPISCOPAL CHURCH.
Van Schaack Memorial Window, Ornamental.
Hibbard Memorial Windows, "Faith," "Our
Saviour."
ST JOHN'S MILITARY SCHOOL CHAPEL.
Damon Memorial Window, Ornamental.
ST. JOHN'S CHURCH.
Verbeck Memorial Window, "St. John the
Evangelist."

Matteawan
ST. LUKE'S EPISCOPAL CHURCH.
Memorial Window, "Apotheosis of St. Luke."

Mt. Kisco
ST. MARK'S CHURCH.
Warren Memorial Windows, "St. John of
Patmus" and "I Am the Resurrection and the
Life."
Bacon Memorial Window, "St. Christopher"
and "The Nativity."

Mt. St. Vincent
CHAPEL OF THE SISTERS OF CHARITY.
Ornamental Windows.
Decorations.

Mt. Vernon
WARTBURG FARM ORPHAN SCHOOL.
Chapel Windows, Ornamental.
Hauslet Memorial Window, "Christ Blessing
Little Children."

Newark
CHURCH OF THE REDEEMER.
Allison Memorial Window, "Angel of
Resurrection."

New Berlin
ST. ANDREW'S EPISCOPAL CHURCH.
Arnold Memorial Window, "Angel of
Resurrection."

New Brighton
CHRIST CHURCH.
Alexander Memorial Window, "Presentation in
Temple."
Schmackenberg Memorial Window, "Christ
Blessing Children."
DeBost Memorial Window, "Resurrection."
Van Vredenberg Memorial Window, "Christ,
Mary and Martha."
Ornamental Windows.

Newburgh
ST. GEORGE'S CHURCH.
Brewster Memorial Window, "Adoration of the
Cross."

New Rochelle
TRINITY EPISCOPAL CHURCH.
Iselin Memorial Window, "The Three Marys at
the Tomb."
Fisher Memorial Window, "Christ and
Charity."
FIRST PRESBYTERIAN CHURCH.
Lester Memorial Window, "Cornelius and
Angel."
Phraner Memorial Window.
Huguenot Memorial Window.

ST. GABRIEL'S ROMAN CATHOLIC CHURCH.
Iselin Commemoration Window, "Marriage of Joseph and Mary."
Iselin Memorial Window, "Education of Virgin."
Kane Memorial Window, "Baptism."

Newtown
CALVARY CEMETERY.
Brown Mausoleum Window, "Angel of the Resurrection."

New Windsor
ST. THOMAS CHURCH.
Ornamental Windows.
Nichol Memorial Window, "Calvary."

North Granville
MEMORIAL CHAPEL.
Comstock Memorial Window, Ornamental.

Northport, L. I.
TRINITY EPISCOPAL CHURCH.
Brown Memorial Window, "Our Saviour."
Parrott Memorial Window, "St. John."
Knight Memorial Window.

Ogdensburg
ST. JOHN'S EPISCOPAL CHURCH.
Knapp Memorial Window, "Faith."
Harriman Memorial Windows, Ornamental and "The Nativity."
Knapp Memorial Window, "Resurrection."
Clark Memorial Windows, "Behold the Lamb of God," and Ornamental.
Mosaic Floor.

Olean
CEMETERY.
Coast Mausoleum, Ornamental.

Oneida
FIRST PRESBYTERIAN CHURCH.
Randall Memorial Window, "I Am the Way, the Truth and the Life."

Ossining
ISLAND AVENUE METHODIST EPIS. CHURCH.
Young Memorial Window, "Christ Enthroned."
TRINITY PROTESTANT EPISCOPAL CHURCH.
Barlow Memorial Window, "The Baptism."
Kane Memorial Window, "Figure of Christ."
McAlpin Memorial Window, "Prodigal Son."
Sing Memorial Windows, "Symbols of Trinity," "The Salutation."
Memorial Windows, "St. Agnes," St. Eulalia" and "St. Euphenia," "Symbols of the Twelve Apostles."

Oswego
CHRIST EPISCOPAL CHURCH.
Ornamental Window, "Lilies."
Clark Memorial Window, "Angel of Resurrection."
PAGE MEMORIAL CHAPEL.
Page Memorial Window, "Resurrection" and Ornamental.
ORPHAN ASYLUM.
Clark Memorial Window, Ornamental.

Peekskill
ST. PETER'S RECTORY.
Lewis Memorial Windows.

Pelham Manor
PRESBYTERIAN CHURCH.
Black Memorial Window, "Education of Virgin."

Portchester
ST. PETER'S EPISCOPAL CHURCH.
Chancel Memorial Window, "Ascension."
Decorations.

Portville
FIRST PRESBYTERIAN CHURCH.
Dusenbury Memorial Window, "Hope."
Wheeler Memorial Window, "Faith."

Potsdam
TRINITY EPISCOPAL CHURCH.
Allen Memorial Window, "Light of the World."
Clarkson Memorial Window, "Good Shepherd."
Usher Memorial Window, "Resurrection Angel."
Clarkson Memorial Windows, "Christian Pathway."
Allen Memorial Window, "Light of the World."
Usher Memorial Window, "Resurrection."
Kirby Memorial Window, "Good Samaritan."

Poughkeepsie
ST. PAUL'S EPISCOPAL CHURCH.
Memorial Window.
Winslow Memorial Window, "The Last Supper."
Ornamental Windows.
CHRIST EPISCOPAL CHURCH.
Gable Windows.
FIRST PRESBYTERIAN CHURCH.
Winslow Memorial Window, "The Last Supper."
VASSAR COLLEGE.
Class Windows Landscape, "Angel of Resurrection" Ornamental Rose Window and Landscape.

Quogue, L. I.
CHURCH OF THE ATONEMENT, EPISCOPAL.
Memorial Window, "Angel of Praise."
Memorial Tablet.
Craig Memorial Window, "Adoring Angels."
CHRIST CHURCH.

Rhinebeck
CHURCH OF THE MESSIAH.
Astor Memorial Window, "Ascension."
Saunders Memorial Window, "Resurrection."

Richfield Springs
PRESBYTERIAN CHURCH.
Ornamental Windows, Chancel Woodwork, Decorations and Furniture.

Rome
ZION EPISCOPAL CHURCH.
Bissell Memorial Window, "Supper at Emmaus."
Brown Memorial Window, "Charity."

Rochester
FIRST PRESBYTERIAN CHURCH.
Pond Memorial Window, "Resurrection Angel."
Hart Memorial Window, "Cherubs."
THIRD PRESBYTERIAN CHURCH.
Hollister Memorial Window, "Angel of the Resurrection."
Oothout Memorial Window, "St. Agnes."
King Memorial Window, "From Cross to Crown."
Loomis Memorial Window, "Angel of Victory."
Oothout Memorial Window, "Holy City."
Stone Memorial Window, landscape.
CALVARY CHURCH.
Graham Memorial Window. Ornamental.
BRICK PRESBYTERIAN CHURCH.
Goesline Memorial Window, "King David."
ST. PAUL'S EPISCOPAL CHURCH.
Woodbury Memorial Window, "Faith, Hope and Charity."
Jones Memorial Window.
Foote Memorial Window, "The Good Shepherd."
Jones Memorial Window, "St. Paul Preaching at Athens."
CHAPEL OF THE CHURCH HOME
(Chapel demolished; windows in storage).
Halsey Memorial Window, "Easter Morning."

Sibley Memorial Window, "Annunciation to Shepherds" and Ornamental.
CHRIST EPISCOPAL CHURCH.
Warren Memorial Window, "Te Deum."
Griffith Memorial Windows, "Nativity" and "Annunciation" and Ornamental.
Weston Memorial Window, Ornamental.
CHURCH OF THE EPIPHANY.
Seymour Memorial Window, "Mary at the Tomb."
FIRST BAPTIST CHURCH.
Cole Memorial Window, "Praise."
ROCHESTER CITY HOSPITAL.
Robinson Memorial Window, "Angel of Praise."
SECURITY TRUST COMPANY.
Ornamental Skylights.
MT. HOPE CEMETERY (all the windows destroyed or removed).
Memorial Windows, "Our Saviour," "St. Agnes," "Magdalen."
Beckley Memorial Window, Ornamental.
Curtis Mausoleum Landscape.
Woodworth Mausoleum, "Angel of Resurrection."
Cook Mausoleum, "Scene in the Black Forest."
G. Curtis Mausoleum, Landscape.
Bissell Memorial Window, "St. Paul Preaching at Athens."
Carhahan Memorial Window, "Faithful Servant."
Gillis Memorial Window, "Good Shepherd."
Jones Memorial Window, "Good Samaritan."

Roundout
ROUNDOUT SYNAGOGUE.
Ornamental Windows.

Roxbury
GOULD MEMORIAL CHAPEL.
Memorial Window, "The Resurrection."
Memorial Window, "Faith, Hope and Charity."

Rye
CHRIST EPISCOPAL CHURCH.
Quintard Memorial Window, "The New Jerusalem."
Ornamental Windows.
Chancel Decorations.
Greer Memorial Window, Medallion.
Wainwright Memorial Window.

Sacketts Harbor
PRESBYTERIAN CHURCH.
Camp Memorial Window, "Jewelled Cross and Crown."
McGoman Memorial Window, "Figure of Christ."

Sag Harbor
CHRIST EPISCOPAL CHURCH.
Belknap Memorial Window, "Cross."

St. James
ST. JAMES EPISCOPAL CHURCH.
Miller Memorial Window, "Good Shepherd."

Salem
ST. PAUL'S EPISCOPAL CHURCH.
Rush Memorial Window, Ornamental.

Saranac Lake
FIRST PRESBYTERIAN CHURCH.
Ornamental Memorial Windows to:
Rev. Alfred Yeoman, D. D.
Rev. Fredrick Frelinghuysen Judd, A. M.
Rev. Robert David Harper, D. D.
Rev. William Pratt Breed, D. D.
Ornamental Windows.
ST. LUKE'S EPISCOPAL CHURCH.
Lake Memorial Window, "Christ and St. Luke."

Saratoga Springs
BETHESDA EPISCOPAL CHURCH.
Marvin Memorial Window, "Archangel Raphael."

SARATOGA CLUB.
  Canfield Memorial Window, Ornamental.

Saugerties
ST. MARY'S ROMAN CATHOLIC
CHURCH.
  *Donovan Memorial Window, "Immaculate
  Conception."*

Sayville, L. I.
ST. ANN'S EPISCOPAL CHURCH.
  *Chancel Windows, "Christ and Adoring
  Angels."*
  Prescott Memorial Tablet.

Scarsdale
ST. JAMES THE LESS, EPISCOPAL
CHURCH.
  Bates Memorial Window, "Cross and Lilies."
  "Crown and Lilies."

Schenectady
UNION COLLEGE.
  Gilmore Memorial Window, Ornamental.

Seneca Falls
TRINITY CHURCH.
  "Christ Blessing Children."
  *Partridge Memorial Window, "Three Marys at
  Tomb."*

Sharon Springs
TRINITY CHURCH.
  *Gardner Memorial Window, "A little Child
  Shall Lead Them."*

Shelter Island
ST. MARY'S EPISCOPAL CHURCH.
  Ornamental Windows.
  Nicholl Memorial Window, Ornamental.

Sing Sing
TRINITY CHURCH.

Southampton, L. I.
ST. ANDREW'S DUNE-BY-THE-SEA
EPISCOPAL CHURCH.
  DeLuze Memorial Window, Ornamental.
  Holbrook Memorial Window, Ornamental.
  *Ismay Memorial Window, "Queen of
  Heaven."*
  Trevor Memorial Window, "Good Shepherd."
  *Russell Memorial Window, "Christ Blessing
  Child."*
  Schieffelin Memorial Window, "St. Margaret."
  Betts Memorial Window, Landscape.
  Cryder Memorial Window, "Sir Galahad."
  *Stephens Memorial Window, "Lead, Kindly
  Light."*
  *Thomas Memorial Window, "Christ Blessing
  Children."*

Spuyten Duyvel
EDGEHILL CHAPEL.
  *Johnson Memorial Window, "From Cross to
  Crown."*

Staatsburg
ST. MARGARET'S CHURCH.
  Ornamental Windows.

Stapleton
LUTHERAN CHURCH.
  Keutven Memorial Window, "Martin Luther."

Stottville, Columbia Co.
ST. BARNABAS EPISCOPAL CHURCH.
  Stott Memorial Window, "Cross and Lilies."

Suffern
CHRIST CHURCH.
  *Hamilton Memorial Window, "Praise Ye the
  Lord."*
CHRIST EPISCOPAL CHURCH.
  Maltbie Memorial Window, Symbolical.
  Suffern Memorial Window, Ornamental.
  Ornamental Windows.

Syracuse
ST. PAUL'S CATHEDRAL.
  *Wood Memorial Window, "The Three Marys
  at the Tomb."*
FOURTH PRESBYTERIAN CHURCH.
  *Candee Memorial Window, "Cornelius and
  Angel."*
UNITARIAN CHURCH.
  *Judson Memorial Window, "New Jerusalem"
  (now in the Everson Museum, Syracuse).*
FIRST PRESBYTERIAN CHURCH.
  Belden Memorial Window, "Te Deum."

Tarrytown
DILLINGHAM CHAPEL.
  Memorial Window, "Cross."
CEMETERY.
  Bishop Mausoleum, "Angels."

Tivoli
"THE CASTLE" CHAPEL (ST. JOHN'S).
ST. PAUL'S CHURCH.
  Livingston Memorial Window, "Landscape."

Tottenville, S. I.
ST. STEPHEN'S EPISCOPAL CHURCH.
  Batchelor Memorial Window.

Troy
ST. PAUL'S EPISCOPAL CHURCH.
  *Fuller Memorial Window, "King David,
  Psalms of David."*
  Thompson Memorial Window, "Annunciation."
  *Painter Memorial Window, "Vision of St.
  John."*
  Ornamental Windows.
  Baptistry.
  Decorations.
  Mosaic Reredos.
  Memorial Window, "St. Barnabas" "Timothy."
  *Thompson Memorial Window, "Christ
  Blessing Children."*
  *Tillinghast Memorial Window, "I am the Way,
  the Truth and the Life."*
FIRST PRESBYTERIAN CHURCH.
  *McMillan Memorial Window, "Angels and
  Christ appearing to Nicodemus."*
ST. JOHN'S EPISCOPAL CHURCH.
  *Wilkinson Memorial Window, "Christ Blessing
  Little Children.*
  Gilbert Memorial Window, "The Resurrection."
  *Knight Memorial Window, "St. John's Vision of
  the Holy City."*
EARL MEMORIAL CHAPEL.
  Ornamental and Figure Windows.
CHURCH OF THE HOLY CROSS.
  Tucker Memorial Window, "Nativity."
EPISCOPAL CHURCH OF THE HOLY
CROSS.
  Warren Memorial Window, "St. John."
ST. JOSEPH'S R. C. CHURCH.
  Ornamental Windows.
LIBRARY OF SUPREME COURT.
  Ingalls Cast Bronze Tablet.
HART MEMORIAL LIBRARY.
  *Hart Memorial Window, "The House of
  Aldus."*
  Doughty Memorial Window, Ornamental.
OAKWOOD CEMETERY.
  Kemp Mausoleum, "Angel of Resurrection."

Tuxedo Park
ST. MARY'S EPISCOPAL CHURCH.
  Breese Memorial Window, "The Pilgrims."
  Memorial Window, "Praise."
  De Rham Memorial Window.
  Carter Memorial Window, Floral.
  Griswold Memorial Window, "Crown of Life."
  Hoffman Memorial Window, "Hope."
ST. LUKE'S MEMORIAL CHURCH
EPISCOPAL.
  Memorial Window, "St. Luke."
  Memorial Window, "Adoring Angels."
  Font, Altar, and Chancel Furniture.

Utica
ST. AGNES ROMAN CATHOLIC
CHURCH.

Ornamental and Figure Windows.
GRACE CHURCH.
  Ornamental.
WESTMINSTER PRESBYTERIAN
CHURCH.
  *Terry Memorial Window, "Christ in House of
  Mary and Martha."*
  Cooper Memorial Window, "Easter Morning."
  *Cooper Memorial Window, "Christ Blessing
  Children."*
MUNSON WILLIAMS MEMORIAL
BUILDING.
  Young and White Memorial, Tablet.
CEMETERY.
  Sanborn Mausoleum, "Head of Christ."

Warwick
DUTCH REFORMED CHURCH.
  *McBurney Memorial Window, "The Valiant
  Woman."*

Washingtonville
MOFFATT LIBRARY.
  Ornamental Window.

Waterloo
FIRST PRESBYTERIAN CHURCH.
  *Spare Memorial Windows, "Faith", "Christ
  Blessing Little Children." "Good Shepherd,"
  "Come Unto Me and Hope", and
  Ornamental.*

Waterville
GRACE EPISCOPAL CHURCH.
  Tower Memorial Window, "Our Saviour."
METHODIST CHURCH.
  *Brainard Memorial Window, "The
  Righteous Shall Receive a Crown of Glory."*

Whitsons
CONGREGATIONAL CHURCH.
  *Law Memorial Window, "Joseph Making
  Himself Known to His Brethren," "Moses in
  the Bulrushes," "Christ Blessing Children,"
  "St. George and the Dragon."*

Williamsbridge
ST. MARY'S CHURCH.
  *Memorial Windows, "Madonna and Child" and
  "St. Joseph" and Ornamental.*

Woodlawn
HOYT MAUSOLEUM.
  Memorial Window, "Resurrection Angel."
RICHARD MAUSOLEUM.
  Ornamental Windows.
WOOD MAUSOLEUM.
  Memorial Window.
PIERSON MAUSOLEUM.
  Ornamental Window.
MATTHEISEN MAUSOLEUM.
  Memorial Window, "Fra Angelica Angels."
KINGSLAND MAUSOLEUM.
  Memorial Window, "Christ the Consoler."
RUSSELL MAUSOLEUM.
  Memorial Window, "Our Saviour."
COE MAUSOLEUM.
  Memorial Window, "Madonna di San Siste."
KNOX MAUSOLEUM.
  Memorial Window.
  "Cross and Crown with Lilies."
WEBB MAUSOLEUM.
  Ornamental Window.
HODENPYL MAUSOLEUM.
  Memorial Window.
FAHNESTOCK MAUSOLEUM.
  Ornamental Window, "Egyptian Symbols."
  Mosaics.
CEMETERY.
  Gruner Mausoleum, "St. Celia."
  Hennon Mausoleum, "Angel of Intercession."
  Mowry Mausoleum, "Angel of Faith."
  Osgood Mausoleum, Landscape.
  Paine Mausoleum, Landscape.
  Payntor Mausoleum, "Angel of Resurrection."
  Spear Mausoleum, "Resurrection."
  Graves Mausoleum, Landscape.
  Graves Mausoleum, Bronze Work.

Goelet Mausoleum, Ornamental.
Huppel Mausoleum, Ornamental.
Perkins Mausoleum, Ornamental.
Roberts Mausoleum, Ornamental.
Sloane Mausoleum, Ornamental.
Wyckoff Mausoleum, Ornamental.

Worthington
WORTHINGTON MEMORIAL CHURCH.
Whitehouse Memorial Window, "St. Michael."

Yonkers
ST. JOSEPH'S SEMINARY CHAPEL,
ROMAN CATHOLIC (Dunwoodie).
Window in Archbishop's Room, "Our Lady of Gaudaloupe."
Decorations of Chapel.
Ornamental Windows.
ST. JOHN'S EPISCOPAL CHURCH.
Bowers Memorial Window.
MOQUETTE CHAPEL.
Ornamental Windows.
ST. ANDREW'S EPISCOPAL CHURCH.
Lowry Memorial Window, "Cherubs' Heads."
Memorial Windows in Chancel, "The Last Supper," "St. George" and "St. Michael."
MT. HOPE CEMETERY.
Holden Mausoleum, Landscape.

ALABAMA
Aniston
CHURCH OF ST. MICHAEL AND ALL ANGELS.
Ornamental Windows.
GRACE PROTESTANT EPISCOPAL CHURCH.
Tyler Memorial Window (Medallion).

Mobile
CHRIST CHURCH.
Memorial Window, "Christ Appearing to Nicodemus."

Selma
FIRST BAPTIST CHURCH.
Keith Memorial Window, "Baptism."

ARKANSAS
Helena
ST. JOHN'S PROTESTANT EPISCOPAL CHURCH.
Hargrave's Memorial Window, "St. John."
Horner Memorial Window, "St. Paul."
Jones Memorial Window, "Angel of Praise."
Lockwood Memorial Window, "Figure of Christ."
Thweatt Memorial Window, Ornamental.
Ornamental Windows.

CALIFORNIA
Los Angeles
FIRST PRESBYTERIAN CHURCH.
Ornamental Windows.
FIRST METHODIST CHURCH.
Lott and Mosier Memorial Windows, "Te Deum Laudamus," 1923.
HOLLYWOOD CEMETERY.
Ginter Mausoleum, Memorial Windows.

Mare Island
ST. PETER'S CHAPEL.
Anderson Memorial Window, "St. George."
Baldwin Memorial Window, "St. Zophiel."
Brown Memorial Window, "Angel Faith, St. Luke and St. Mark."
Admiral Capps' Memorial Window, "St. Uriel."
Colhoun Memorial Window, "Truth."
Danenhawser Memorial Window, "Ezekiel."
Fulton Memorial Window, "Hope."
Dupont Memorial Window, "St. Paul."
Gilles Memorial Window, "Sir Galahad."
Gregory Memorial Window, "St. Matthew."
Johnson Memorial Window, "St. Philip."
Mason Memorial Window, "Angel of Resurrection."

Messersmith Memorial Window, "Angel of Charity."
Rice Memorial Window, "St. Paul."
Selfridge Memorial Window, "St. Thomas."
Stephens Memorial Window, "Christ Sustaining Peter."
Turner Memorial Window, "St. Joseph."
Williams Memorial Window, "John the Baptist."
Woods Memorial Window, "Our Lady."
Baldwin Memorial Tablet.

Pasadena
ALL SAINTS' CHURCH.
Ornamental Windows.
Memorial Window, "Christ and Apostles."
Carroll Memorial Window, "Good Shepherd and Angels of Goodness and Mercy."
Evans Memorial Window, "Angel of Faith."
McCormick Memorial Window, Landscape.
Memorial Windows, "Four Evangelists," St. Peter, St. Gregory, St. Augustine, St. Paul, St. Ambrose, St. Jerome and Symbols.
FIRST METHODIST EPISCOPAL CHURCH.
Bailey Memorial Window, "Rose Window."

Redlands
FIRST CONGREGATIONAL CHURCH.
Kingsbury Memorial Window, "Figure of Christ."

San Francisco
CHURCH OF THE ADVENT.
Memorial Window, "Second Advent," Matthew, Mark, Luke and John, Crucifixion, Nativity, Ascension, Triumphant, Militant, Expectant.
MARIA KIPP ORPHANAGE.
Buckingham Memorial Window, "Christ Blessing Children."
CYPRESS LAWN CEMETERY.
Leroker Mausoleum, Ornamental.
Erwin Mausoleum, Figure (destroyed).
LAUREL HILL CEMETERY.
Oelrichs Mausoleum, Landscape (transferred to Odd Fellows Cemetery, San Mateo).
MAUSOLEUM.
Crocker Mausoleum, Window.

San Mateo
CYPRESS LAWN CEMETERY.
Fuller Mausoleum, "Christ Blessing Children" (smashed). Angel of Peace and Landscape.
Kohl Mausoleum, "They shall be mine, Saith the Lord."

San Raphael
ST. MARY'S CHAPEL.
Lily Memorial Window, "St. John the Evangelist."

COLORADO
Cold Springs
ST. STEPHEN'S EPISCOPAL CHURCH.
Ripley Memorial Window, "Christ Child."

Colorado Springs
FIRST CONGREGATIONAL CHURCH.
Hastings Memorial Window, Ornamental.
METHODIST CHURCH.
Barber Memorial Window, "Angel and Child."
NEW METHODIST CHURCH.
Scott Memorial Window, "Christ Blessing Children."

Denver
ST. JOHN'S CATHEDRAL, EPISCOPAL.
Baxter Memorial Window Ornamental.
ST. LEO'S CATHOLIC CHURCH
(demolished late 1970s).
Memorial Windows on Life of Christ.
Over Choir Gallery, Harp with Angel Face.
CENTRAL PRESBYTERIAN CHURCH.
General Glass.

Pueblo
FIRST CONGREGATIONAL CHURCH.
Ornamental Windows.

CONNECTICUT
Ansonia
FIRST CONGREGATIONAL CHURCH.
Markwick Memorial Window, "St. John."

Bethel
ST. MARY'S CHURCH.
O'Connell Memorial Window, Symbols of Sacred Heart.
ST. THOMAS CHURCH.
Hansy Memorial Window, "Come Unto Me."
Ferry Memorial, "Adoring Angels."

Birmingham
ST. JAMES EPISCOPAL CHURCH.
Memorial Window, "Guardian Angel."
Memorial Window, "Presentation in the Temple."

Branford
TRINITY CHURCH.
Young Memorial Window, "Angel of Thanksgiving."

Bridgeport
FIRST METHODIST CHURCH.
Ferris Memorial Window, Ornamental.
SMITH MAUSOLEUM.
Mausoleum Building.
Memorial Window, "The Pilgrims."
Ornamental Windows.
Furnishings and Fittings.
ST. LUKE'S EPISCOPAL CHURCH.
Beach Memorial Window, Landscape and Cross.
SECOND BAPTIST CHURCH.
Black Memorial, "Christ and Four Evangelists."
ST. JOHN'S CHURCH.
Pettingill Memorial Tablet.

Brooklyn
TRINITY CHURCH.
Jarvis Memorial Window, "Floral."
Marlor Memorial Window, "Benedictus."
Welch Memorial Window, Ornamental.

Clinton
CONGREGATIONAL CHURCH.
Ornamental Windows.

Danbury
FIRST CONGREGATIONAL CHURCH.
Benedict Memorial Window, "Christ and His Disciples on the way to Emmaus."
SECOND BAPTIST CHURCH.
Hull and Gregory Memorial Window, "Christ in the Temple."
Memorial Window, "The Emancipation."
Fairchild Memorial Window, "Boy Christ in the Temple."
Ornamental Windows.
Armstrong Memorial Window, "Lord is my Shepherd."
CONGREGATIONAL CHURCH.
Cook Memorial Window, "The Sower."
ST. JAMES' PROTESTANT EPISCOPAL CHURCH.
Wile Memorial Window, "Ascension."
CHURCH OF THE DISCIPLES.
General Glass.

E. Haddam
ST. STEPHEN'S CHURCH.
Atwood Memorial Tablet.

Fairfield
ST. PAUL'S EPISCOPAL CHURCH.
Memorial Window.
CHRIST CHURCH.
Child Memorial Window, Medallion.
Jennings Memorial Window, "Scenes from Life of Christ."

Falls Village
METHODIST EPISCOPAL CHURCH.
Spurr Memorial Window, "Charity."
Gaylor Memorial Window, Ornamental.

Glastonbury
ST. JAMES' CHURCH.
Kingsbury Memorial Window, Ornamental.

Greenwich
CHRIST EPISCOPAL CHURCH.
Memorial Window, "King's Daughters."
Johnson Memorial Window, "Resurrection."
*Barrett Memorial Window, "Christ Blessing
Little Children."*
FIRST PRESBYTERIAN CHURCH.
Martin Memorial Window, "Cherubs."

Grotham
CONGREGATIONAL CHURCH.
*Woodhull Memorial Window, "The Lord is my
Shepherd."*

Hartford
ST. JAMES EPISCOPAL CHURCH.
Memorial Window, "Cross and Anchor."
FIRST CONGREGATIONAL CHURCH.
Smith Memorial Window, "St. John."
*Parsons Memorial Window, "Resurrection
Angel."*
Nooker Memorial Window, "Hope."
CENTER CHURCH.
Hooker Memorial Window.
*Wells Memorial Window, "Righteousness and
Peace."*
SO. PARK METHODIST EPISCOPAL
CHURCH.
Munsill Memorial Window, "Angel of Faith."
WADSWORTH MUSEUM.
Ornamental Windows.
HARTFORD HOSPITAL.
Beresford Memorial Window "Æsculapius."
CEDAR HILL CEMETERY.
Valentine Mausoleum, "Faith."

Lakeville
CHAPEL OF HOTCHKISS SCHOOL
(demolished in 1952; whereabouts of
windows unknown).
*Buehler Memorial Window, "Landscape and
Sunset."*
Goss Memorial Window, Ornamental.
Mager Memorial Window, Ornamental.

Litchfield
ST. MICHAEL'S EPISCOPAL CHURCH.
*Hornblower Memorial Window, "Ascension
Lillies."*
Latimer Memorial Window, "St. Michael."
FIRST CONGREGATIONAL CHURCH.
Buel Memorial Window, "Good Shepherd."

Meriden
ST. ANDREW'S EPISCOPAL CHURCH.
Dodd Memorial Window.
Squire Memorial Window, "Annunciation."
ST. PAUL'S UNIVERSALIST CHURCH.
Chapin Memorial Window, "The Sower."
Mosaic Pulpit.

Middletown
ST. JOHN'S CHURCH.
Ornamental Windows.
YOUNG MEN'S CHRISTIAN
ASSOCIATION.
Ornamental Windows.

Milford
ST. PETER'S EPISCOPAL CHURCH.
Peck Memorial Window.
PUBLIC LIBRARY.
Smith Memorial Window.

Monroe
ST. PETER'S EPISCOPAL CHURCH.
Beardsley Memorial Window, Ornamental.

New Britain
SOUTH CONGREGATIONAL CHURCH.
Stanley Memorial Window, Ornamental.
Woodruff Memorial Window, Ornamental.
*Boardman Memorial Window, "Angel of
Purity."*

ALL SOULS' CONGREGATIONAL
CHURCH.
Cooper Memorial Window.
ST. MARY'S CHURCH.
*Memorial Windows: Holy Family, Boy Christ,
St. Joseph, Blessed Virgin Mary, 12 Apostles,
Return of the Prodigal, Mary Magdalen at Feet
of Christ, Charge to Peter, Good Shepherd.*

New Haven
CENTER CHURCH.
*English Memorial Window, "Illust. Malachi
4–17."*
*Pratt Memorial Window, "Angel of
Resurrection."*
Trowbridge Memorial Window, Landscape.
Trowbridge Memorial Window, Historical.
*now in the Southern Connecticut State
College
*Trowbridge Memorial Window, "John
Davenport Preaching to the Colonists of New
Haven."*
GRAND AVENUE CONGREGATIONAL
CHURCH.
Perkins Memorial Window, "Come Unto Me."
TRINITY PROTESTANT EPISCOPAL
CHURCH.
*Wade Memorial Window, "St. Paul at
Athens."*
Barnes Memorial Window, "Easter Morning."
*Memorial Window, "Christ on the Road to
Emmaus."*
FAIR HAVEN UNION CEMETERY
CHAPEL.
*Thompson Memorial Windows, "St. Luke" and
"Faith."*
*Strong Memorial Window, "Law, Fortitude and
Temperance."*
Bennett Memorial Window, "St. Cecilia."
UNITED CHURCH.
NEW HAVEN HOUSE.
ST. THOMAS EPISCOPAL CHURCH.
Mansfield Memorial Window, "St. Cecilia."
Heaton Memorial Window, "St. John."
BATTELL CHAPEL, YALE COLLEGE.
Williams Memorial Window.
CHITTENDEN LIBRARY, YALE COLLEGE
(the library is now used as a classroom).
Chittenden Memorial Window, "Education."
WOLF'S HEAD SOCIETY BUILDING.
Ornamental Windows and Decorations.

New London
ST. JAMES' PROTESTANT EPISCOPAL
CHURCH.
Allun Memorial, "The Holy Family."
Loomis Memorial, "Annunciation to Mary."
*Memorial Window, "St. Francis and St.
Joseph and St. Sebastian."*
*Whittlesey Memorial, "Annunciation to the
Shepherds."*
Ironside Memorial.
Williams Memorials, "Truth" and "Justice."

New Milford
ALL SAINTS' EPISCOPAL CHURCH.
*Black Memorial Window, "Old and New
Dispensations."*
*Sanford Memorial Window, "The Three
Marys at the Tomb."*
Ornamental Windows.
CONGREGATIONAL CHURCH.
Hine Memorial Window, "Faith."

Newington
ST. JAMES EPISCOPAL CHURCH.
Miller Memorial Window.

Norfolk
CHURCH OF CHRIST
CONGREGATIONAL, BATTELL
CHAPEL.
Stoeckel Memorials.

Norwich
BROADWAY CONGREGATIONAL
CHURCH.
Ornamental Windows.
Decorations.

Pequot, New London
PEQUOT CHAPEL.
*Woodward Memorial Window, "Adoring
Angels."*

Pomfret
CHRIST EPISCOPAL CHURCH.
Vinton Memorial Windows.

Rockville
UNION CONGREGATIONAL CHURCH.
Memorial Window.

Salisbury
CONGREGATIONAL CHURCH.
Marble Tablet.
SCOVILLE MEMORIAL LIBRARY.
Scoville Memorial Tablet.

Saybrook
GRACE EPISCOPAL CHURCH.
*Bishop McKnight Memorial Window,
Ornamental.*

Shelton
CHURCH OF GOOD SHEPHERD.
*Burr Memorial Window, "Good Shepherd" and
Symbols of Four Evangelists.*

Simsbury
METHODIST EPISCOPAL CHURCH.
*Ebsign Memorial, "Christ Blessing Children"
and Ornamental Windows.*

So. Manchester
EPISCOPAL CHURCH.
*Cheney Memorial Window, "Angel of
Resurrection" and Chancel.*

Southport
PUBLIC LIBRARY.
Holman Memorial Window, Ornamental.

Stamford
FIRST PRESBYTERIAN CHURCH.
Memorial Window, "Figure of Christ."
ST. JOHN'S CHURCH.
*Davenport Memorial Window, "Figure of
Christ."*
*Smith Memorial Window, "Moses and
Joshua."*
Leeds Memorial Window, "Transfiguration."
Smith Memorial, Tablet.
Tatlock Memorial, Tablet.
ST. LUKE'S CHAPEL OF ST. JOHN'S
CHURCH.
St. Luke," Memorial Window.

Waterbury
SECOND CONGREGATIONAL CHURCH
(demolished).
*Chase Memorial Window, "Christ Blessing
Children."*
TRINITY EPISCOPAL CHURCH.
Perry Memorial Window, "Annunciation."
*Young Memorial Window, "Angels of
Adoration."*
ST. JOHN'S PROTESTANT EPISCOPAL
CHURCH.
Kingsbury Memorial Window.
Merriman Memorial Window, "St. Simeon."
Poore Memorial Window, "Call of Matthew."
Driggs Memorial Window, "Te Deum."

West Hartford
ST. JAMES EPISCOPAL.
Coffing Memorial Window, Ornamental.

Westport
CHRIST EPISCOPAL CHURCH.
*Bull Memorial Window, "Christ
Commissioning His Disciples."*
*Bouton Memorial Window, "Three Marys at
Tomb."*
FIRST PROTESTANT EPISCOPAL
CHURCH.
*Putnam Memorial Window, "Matthew
28–18, 19 and 20."*

Westville
ST. JAMES EPISCOPAL CHURCH.
Chancel Window, Ornamental.

Wethersfield
TRINITY EPISCOPAL CHURCH.
Memorial Window, Ornamental.

Winsted
SECOND CONGREGATIONAL CHURCH.
Boyd Memorial Window, "Landscape."
*Gay Memorial Window, "Lord is my
Shepherd."*
Holmes Memorial, mosaic plaque.

Woodbury
ST. PAUL'S CHURCH.
*Peck Memorial Window, Ornamental with
Cross.*

Woodstock
CONGREGATIONAL CHURCH.
Billings Memorial Window, Ornamental.
CHURCH OF ST. JAMES THE GREAT.
Smith Memorial Window, "St. James."

DELAWARE
Wilmington
TRINITY EPISCOPAL CHURCH.
Mealey Memorial Window, "St. Agnes."
Cook Memorial Window, "St. Ann."
Ware Memorial Window, "Faith."
*Armstrong Memorial Window, "While
Shepherds watched their flocks at night."*
Salsbury Memorial Window, "Come Unto Me."
Wilson Memorial Window, "Compassion."
OLD SWEDES EPISCOPAL CHURCH.
Memorial Window.

DISTRICT OF COLUMBIA
Rock Creek
SOLDIERS' HOME.
*Memorial Window, "Honor Thy Father and
Thy Mother."*
CEMETERY.
Wilkins Mausoleum, "Return of Soul."

Tacoma Park
CHURCH OF REDEEMER.
Ornamental Windows.

Washington
ST. PAUL'S EPISCOPAL CHURCH.
Ornamental Windows.
"St. James."
ST. PAUL'S EPISCOPAL CHURCH,
(SOLDIERS HOME, ROCK CREEK).
*Hubbard Memorial Window, "Madonna and
Child."*
ST. MARK'S EPISCOPAL CHURCH.
*Lander Memorial Window, "Christ Leaving the
Praetorium."*
EPIPHANY CHAPEL.
McKim Memorial Window.
Ornamental Windows.
GUNTON TEMPLE MEMORIAL CHURCH.
Ornamental Windows.
Decorations.
ALL SOUL'S CHURCH.
*Memorial Window, "Christ Blessing Little
Children."*
CENTRAL PRESBYTERIAN CHURCH.
*Busey Memorial Window, "Sky, Dove and
Jewelled Cross."*
THE AMERICAN RED CROSS
HEADQUARTERS, ASSEMBLY HALL
*Women's Relief Corps and United Daughters of
the Confederacy Memorial.*
FIRST BAPTIST CHURCH.
ST. JOHN'S EPISCOPAL CHURCH.
Rittenhouse Memorial Window, "Lilies."
CHURCH OF THE COVENANT.
*Strong Memorial Window, "Paying of
Tribute."*
*Strong Memorial Window, "Angel of
Resurrection."*
Ornamental Windows.

ST. MARGARET CHURCH.
*Memorial Window, "Christ on Road to
Emmaus."*
ASSEMBLY METHODIST CHURCH.
Ornamental Windows.
ST. MARY'S PROTESTANT EPISCOPAL
CHURCH.
Memorial Window, "Angel of Peace."
ST. PETER'S CHURCH.
*O'Brien Memorial Windows, "Crucifixion,"
"St. Peter," "St. Paul," "St. Patrick," "St.
Columbo."*
Ornamental Windows.
ST. PAUL'S ROMAN CATHOLIC
CHURCH.
Rose Window, Ornamental.
CHURCH OF THE EPIPHANY.
Arms Memorial Window, "Landscape."
SMITHSONIAN INSTITUTION.
Ornamental Windows.
NATIONAL TRAINING SCHOOL FOR
BOYS.
*Noyes Memorial Window, "Lord is my
Shepherd."*
WHITE HOUSE.
Ornamental Windows.
Decorations.
ARNO HOTEL.
Ornamental Windows.
ARLINGTON HOTEL.
Ornamental Windows.
CEMETERY.
Pinchot Mausoleum, Ornamental.

FLORIDA
Jacksonville
ST. JOHN'S EPISCOPAL CHURCH.
*Ambler Memorial Window, "The Good
Shepherd."*

Lake Worth
EPISCOPAL CHURCH OF BETHESDA-
BY-THE-SEA.
Goss Memorial Window, "Ascension Angel."

Port Orange
GRACE EPISCOPAL CHURCH.
*Meeker Memorial Window, "The Good
Shepherd."*
Meeker Memorial Window, "St. Luke."

Punta Gorda
ST. EDMUND'S EPISCOPAL CHURCH.
*Colt Memorial Window, "The Good
Shepherd."*

St. Augustine
TRINITY PARISH.
*Hewson Memorial Window, "Cornelius and the
Angel."*
PONCE DE LEON HOTEL (now Flagler
College).
Decorations.
Ornamental Windows.

GEORGIA
Atlanta
ALL SAINT'S CHURCH.
Farland Memorial Window, "Annunciation."
NORTH AVENUE PRESBYTERIAN
CHURCH.
Harris Memorial Window, "Christ in Temple."
*High Memorial Window, "Christ Blessing
Children."*
ATLANTA UNIVERSITY.
DuBois Memorial Window, Ornamental.

Augusta
ST. PAUL'S CHURCH.
Baker Memorial Window, "Charity."
FIRST BAPTIST CHURCH.
Memorial Window.

Macon
ST. PAUL'S EPISCOPAL CHURCH.
Crutchfield Memorial Window.

Jackson Memorial Window.

Savannah
CHRIST CHURCH.
Memorial Window.

ILLINOIS
Chicago
CHRIST REFORMED EPISCOPAL
CHURCH, 2nd Street and Michigan
Avenue.
Ornamental Windows.
CHRIST CHURCH, corner Michigan
Avenue and 24th Street (demolished in 1962).
Fisher Memorial Window, "St. Luke."
Fuller Memorial Window, "Angel."
Aldrich Memorial Window.
Cory Memorial Window, Ornamental, "Lilies."
Ornamental Windows.
ST. PETER'S EPISCOPAL CHURCH.
*McDonald Memorial Window, "Resurrection
Angel."*
CHURCH OF THE EPIPHANY.
Memorial Window (destroyed in 1968).
CHURCH OF OUR SAVIOUR.
Beunt, "Blessing Children."
FIRST PRESBYTERIAN CHURCH, 21st
Street and Indiana Avenue (windows given
to Second Presbyterian).
Humphrey Memorial Window, Ornamental.
*Mitchell Memorial Window, "St. Paul
Preaching at Athens."*
SECOND PRESBYTERIAN CHURCH, 20th
Street and Michigan Avenue.
*Kellogg Memorial Window, "Angel of
Adoration."*
*Spencer Memorial Window, "Christ Blessing
Little Children."*
*Fargo Memorial Window, "Angel of
Resurrection."*
*Balcom Memorial Window, "Behold, the Lamb
of God."*
Curtiss Memorial Window, "Transfiguration."
Ornamental Windows.
CENTENNIAL BAPTIST CHURCH
(demolished).
*Griffin Memorial Window, "Lydia Entertaining
Christ and Apostles."*
*Rundel Memorial Window, "Lilies and
Passion Flowers."*
HYDE PARK BAPTIST CHURCH.
Harper Memorial Window, "Amos and Hosiah."
HYDE PARK PRESBYTERIAN CHURCH.
*Llewellyn Memorial Window, "Good
Shepherd."*
KENWOOD EVANGELIST CHURCH.
Carton Memorial Window, "The Child Christ."
Spooner Memorial Window, "St. John."
TRINITY EPISCOPAL (burnt down in 1920).
Blair Memorial Window, "Ascension."
Sargent Memorial Tablet.
ST. JAMES EPISCOPAL CHURCH.
*Hopkins Memorial Window, "Resurrection
Angel."*
ST. JAMES' ROMAN CATHOLIC
CHURCH (windows shattered in 1970).
*Memorial Window, "Annunciation,"
"Transfiguration," and "Nativity,"
Ornamental Windows.*
CHICAGO UNIVERSITY.
Ornamental Windows.
ART INSTITUTE.
Memorial Room, Ornamental Glass.
LAKEVIEW HIGH SCHOOL.
*Bathwick Memorial Window, "St. Martin and
St. Raphael."*
CHICAGO PUBLIC LIBRARY.
*Mosaic and Decorations in Washington Street
Entrance and Delivery Room.*
*Painting and Decoration in Reading and
Reference Room (The Room redecorated).*
CHICAGO CLUB.
Ornamental Windows.
LASALLE HOTEL (closed in 1977).
Ornamental Windows.
FULLERTON HALL.
Ornamental Windows.

ROSENBAUM MEMORIAL BUILDING.
Memorial Window, "Truth."

Evanston
FIRST PRESBYTERIAN CHURCH.
Keppler Memorial Window.

Kenwood
KENWOOD EVANGELICAL CHURCH.
Atwood Memorial Window.

Knoxville
ST. MARY'S SCHOOL.
Leffingwell Memorial Window, "St. Margaret."

Lagrange
EMMANUEL EPISCOPAL CHURCH.
Chancel Furnishings.
Decorations.

Lake Forest
FIRST PRESBYTERIAN CHURCH.
Williams Memorial Window, "Faith."
Smith Memorial Window, "I am the way, the truth and the life."
Reid Memorial Window, "Angel of Prayer."
Durand Memorial Window, "Resurrection."
REID MEMORIAL CHAPEL (destroyed by fire in 1940).
Reid Memorial Window, "Landscape."
LAKE FROST ACADEMY.
Reid Memorial Window, "Boy Christ."

Peoria
ST. PAUL'S EPISCOPAL CHURCH.
Nave Windows, SS. Paul and Peter.
      SS. James and Andrew.
      SS. Matthew, Mark, Luke and John.
Gable Windows, "Nativity," "Baptism," "Resurrection" and "Ascension."

Quincy
FIRST UNION CONGREGATIONAL CHURCH.
White Memorial Window, "The Good Shepherd."
Ornamental Windows.
Decorations.

Rock Island
CEMETERY.
Dankman Mausoleum, "River of Life."

Springfield
FIRST PRESBYTERIAN CHURCH.
McKee Memorial Window, "Angel of Resurrection."
Ferguson Memorial Window, "Angel of Victory."
Rose Window, "Holy Spirit."
Ornamental Windows.
Bunn Memorial Window, "St. John."
Brown Memorial Window, "St. Barnabas."
Stuve Memorial Window, "Angel with Cherubs."

Waukegan
CHRIST EPISCOPAL CHURCH.
Parks Memorial Window.

INDIANA
Indianapolis
MERIDIAN STREET METHODIST CHURCH.
Stewart Memorial Window, "Resurrection Angel."
Ornamental Window.
SECOND PRESBYTERIAN CHURCH (moved from downtown to Meridian Street in 1960s).
Ornamental Windows and Decorations.
Sayles Memorial Window, "The Ascension with Passion Flower and Vine."
FIRST PRESBYTERIAN CHURCH.
President Harrison Memorial Window, "St.

Michael" (now in the Indianapolis Museum of Art).
JACKSON INSTITUTE.
Hanna Memorial Tablet.
CEMETERY.
Dickson Mausoleum, "Light of the World."
Knight Mausoleum, "Return of the Soul."

Marion
FIRST PRESBYTERIAN CHURCH.
Prestice Memorial Tablet.
Sweetser Memorial Window, "St. Agnes."

Rangoon
AMERICAN BAPTIST MISSIONARY UNION.
Memorial Window, "Figure of Christ."

Richmond
ST. PAUL'S PROTESTANT EPISCOPAL CHURCH.
Jackson Memorial Window, "Angel of the Resurrection."
REID MEMORIAL CHURCH.
Glass Memorial Window, "Resurrection."
Reid Memorial Windows, "Christ and the Four Evangelists," "Finding the Boy Christ in the Temple."
Fixtures.
MORRISON PUBLIC LIBRARY.
Morrison Memorial Window, "Guttenberg and the Early Printers."

South Bend
ST. JAMES EPISCOPAL CHURCH.
Studebaker Memorial Window, Ornamental.
Foote Memorial Window, Ornamental.
Meyer Memorial Window, Ornamental.
Chancel Window, "St. James."
CEMETERY.
Studebaker Mausoleum, "Angel of the Resurrection."

IOWA
Cedar Rapids
GRACE CHURCH.
Green Memorial Window, Figure.
Memorial Windows, "St. Cecilia," "Madonna and Child," "St. Catherine," "St. Agnes," "St. Margaret," "Transfiguration," Ornamental Windows.

Council Bluffs
ST. PAUL'S EPISCOPAL CHURCH.
Stewart Memorial Window, "Angel of Prayer."

Dubuque
ST. JOHN'S EPISCOPAL CHURCH.
Peabody Memorial Window.
Seymour Memorial Window.
Coyningham Memorial Window.
Daniels Memorial Window, "Prayers of the Shepherd."
Peabody Memorial Window, "Charity."
CONGREGATIONAL CHURCH.
O'Donnell Memorial Window, "Angel of Victory."
ST. LUKE'S METHODIST CHURCH.
Cooley Memorial Window, "The Good Shepherd."
Richardson Memorial Window, "Resurrection Angel."
Hancock Memorial Window, "Angel of Victory."
Staples Memorial Window, "Ascension."
Farley Memorial Window, "Job."
Ornamental Windows.

Iowa City
CONGREGATIONAL CHURCH.
Ornamental Window.

KANSAS
Atchinson
TRINITY CHURCH.
Drury Memorial Window, "Praise."

Fort Riley
CHAPEL.
Bronze Memorial Tablet.

Leavenworth
FIRST PRESBYTERIAN CHURCH.
Wilson Memorial Window, "Come Unto Me."

KENTUCKY
Covington
TRINITY PROTESTANT EPISCOPAL CHURCH.
Laurel Memorial Window, "Blessed Are the Pure in Heart."

Hopkinsville
CEMETERY.
Latham Mausoleum, "Figure of Hope."

Lexington
LEXINGTON CEMETERY CHAPEL.
Bell Memorial Window, "St. Joseph and Infant Christ."

Louisville
CHRIST CHURCH CATHEDRAL, EPISCOPAL.
Ballard Memorial Window, "Angel of Praise."
Ten Broeck Memorial Window, "Good Samaritan."
Craik Memorial Window, "Resurrection Angel."
Dudley Memorial Window, Ornamental.
McCulloch Memorial Window, "Resurrection."
CHURCH OF THE SACRED HEART, ROMAN CATHOLIC.
Byrne Memorial Window, "Sacred Heart."
Disney Memorial Window, "The Good Shepherd."
CALVARY CHURCH.
Hogan Memorial Window, "Charity."
Taylor Memorial Window, "In My Father's House Are Many Mansions."
TRINITY METHODIST EPISCOPAL CHURCH.
Dugan Memorial Window, "Lilies."

LOUISIANA
Baton Rouge
ST. JAMES CHURCH.
Connell Memorial Window, "Angel of Resurrection."

New Orleans
CHAPEL OF THE H. SOPHIE NEWCOMB MEMORIAL COLLEGE.
Newcomb Memorial Window, "The Resurrection."
Le Monnier Memorial Window, "St. Cecilia," "King David."
Ornamental. Rose Window.
Newcomb Memorial Window, "Good Samaritan."
RICHARD MILIKEN MEMORIAL HOSPITAL.
Miliken Memorial Window, "Landscape."
TILTON MEMORIAL LIBRARY.
Tilton Memorial Window, "Art and Literature" (now in the Business Administration Building).
NEWCOMB MEMORIAL COLLEGE.
Callender Memorial Window, "Supper at Emmaus."

MAINE
Alfred
CONGREGATIONAL CHURCH.
Memorial Window, Ornamental.

Augusta
FIRST CONGREGATIONAL CHURCH (now the South Parish Congregational Church).
Morrill Memorial Window, "St. John."

Milliken Memorial Window, "Angel of Praise."
Haines Memorial Window, "Faith."
Stanwood Memorial Window, "King David."
Emmons Blaine Memorial Window, "24th Psalm."
James G. Blaine Memorial Window, Ornamental.
Bradbury Memorial Window, "Madonna."
J. G. Blain Memorial Window, "St. Luke."
Johnson Memorial Window, "Charity."
Dorr Memorial, "Christ knocking at the Door."
Sturgis Memorial.
ST. MARK'S PROTESTANT EPISCOPAL CHURCH.
Marble Memorial Window, "Ascension."

Bangor
ST. JOHN'S CHURCH (original building burnt down in 1911).
Gibson Memorial Window, "Easter Lilies and Angel of Resurrection."
French Memorial Window.
Thissel Memorial Window, "Faith."
Memorial Window, "The Boy Christ."
CENTRAL CONGREGATIONAL CHURCH.
Steinbach Memorial Window, "Christ Washing Disciples Feet."
Dennett Memorial Window, "Christ and Charity."
FIRST CONGREGATIONAL CHURCH.
Bowler Memorial Window, Ornamental with Grape Vine.
FIRST BAPTIST CHURCH.
Whittier Memorial Window, "Ascension."
HAMILTON CONGREGATIONAL CHURCH.
Ayers Memorial Window, "Faith and Hope."

Bar Harbor
ST. SAVIOUR'S EPISCOPAL CHURCH.
Lyon Memorial Window.
Chancel Window, "The Last Supper."
Reed Memorial Window, "Fra Angelica Angel."
Smith Memorial Window, "Flight into Egypt."
Gordon Memorial Window, "Angel of Praise."
Burnham Memorial Window, Ornamental.
Hauge Memorial Window, 'Salve Regina."
Washington Memorial
Joy Memorial.

Bath
CEMETERY.
Morse Mausoleum, "Angel of Faith."

Fairfield
GOOD WILL HOME.
Ryerson Memorial Window, Ornamental.

Hinckley
WHITNEY HOME.
McGregor Memorial Tablet.

Hulls Cove
CHURCH OF OUR FATHER.
Parsons Memorial, "Resurrection," 1920s.

Kennebunkport
CONGREGATIONAL CHURCH.
Clark Memorial Window, Ornamental.

Portland
CENTRAL CONGREGATIONAL CHURCH.
Brown Memorial Window, "Baptism of Christ."

Sorento
CHAPEL.
Lamonte Memorial Tablet.
Fuller Memorial Tablet.

Waterville
WATERVILLE UNIVERSITY.
Memorial Tablet.

Winter Harbor
EPISCOPAL CHURCH.

Trotter Memorial Window, "Christ Healing Peter's Wife's Mother."
ST. CHRISTOPHER'S CHURCH.
Landreth Memorial Window, "Cherubs," "Heads."

MARYLAND
Annapolis
ST. ANN'S EPISCOPAL CHURCH.
Sand Memorial Window, "St. Anne and the Blessed Virgin Mary."
UNITED STATES NAVAL ACADEMY.
Sampson Memorial Window, "Angel of Peace."
Mason Memorial Window, "Christian Soldier."
Phelps Memorial Window.
Porter Memorial Window, "Christ Walking on Water."
CADET QUARTERS.
Ornamental Windows.
MARYLAND STATE BUILDING.
Ornamental Windows and Skylights.

Baltimore
ST. PAUL'S EPISCOPAL CHURCH, Charles & W. Saratoga Streets.
Bishop Whittingham Memorial Window, "St. Augustine and His Mother."
Ornamental Windows.
Bonsal Memorial Window, "Three Marys at Tomb."
Chatard Memorial Window, "Angel of Faith."
Mayer Memorial Window, "Faith."
Pennington Window, "Hope."
Potts Memorial Window, "St. Luke."
Williams Memorial Window, "Benediction."
Wyatt Window, Ornamental with "Christ's Head."
EMMANUEL EPISCOPAL CHURCH.
Wade Memorial Window, "Christ Blessing Little Children."
Gosnell Memorial Window, "Angel and Child."
Ornamental Windows.
Latrobe Memorial Window, "Nicodemus."
MT. CALVARY EPISCOPAL CHURCH.
Memorial Window, "The Good Shepherd."
FIRST INDEPENDENT CHRIST CHURCH.
Chancel Window, Ornamental.
Mosaic Reredos Panel, "The Last Supper."
Decorations.
Sedalia and Chairs.
Ornamental Windows.
FIRST PRESBYTERIAN CHURCH, Madison Street and Park Avenue.
Canfield Memorial Window, "Gethsemane."
Spence Memorial Window, "Jesus at the Well."
GRACE EPISCOPAL CHURCH (combined with St. Peter's).
Middleton Memorial Window, "Daughter of Jairus."
THE REFORMED CHURCH (now the Annunciation Greek Orthodox Cathedral).
Ball Memorial Window, "Sermon on the Mount."
Leybum Memorial Tablet.
CHRIST EPISCOPAL CHURCH.
Memorial Window, "The Ascension."
Nelson Memorial Windows, "Christ in Carpenter Shop," "Christ Preaching in the Temple," "Christ Walking on the Water," "Peter and John."
MASONIC TEMPLE (destroyed by fire).
Stair Window, "Silence."
Asylum Window, Heraldic Design.
Ornamental Windows.
TEMPLE OHEB SHOLEM, Eutaw Place and Lanvale Street.
Ornamental Windows.
ASSOCIATE CONGREGATIONAL CHURCH (now the Annunciation Greek Orthodox Cathedral).
Huckle Memorial Window, "Christ Knocking at Door," "Christ the Consoler."
Stockbridge Memorial Window, "Good Shepherd."
BROWN MEMORIAL CHURCH.
Hanway Memorial Window, "Christ Walking on Water."

Wilson Memorial Window, "St. Gabriel."
Von Lingen Memorial Window, "St. John."
Stone Memorial Window, "Gethsemane."
McCormick Memorial Window, "Come Unto Me."
Kerr Memorial Window, "Lead Kindly Light."
Hoffman Memorial Windows, "Praise," "Christ Blessing Children," "Annunciation to Shepherds," "Holy City."
HENSHAW MEMORIAL CHURCH (destroyed by fire in 1932; now St. Paul the Apostle).
Kelso Memorial Window, "Cross and Crown."
ST. MARK'S LUTHERAN CHURCH.
Ornamental Window.
ST. PETER'S CHURCH (combined in 1912 with Grace Church).
Hurst Window, "A New Commandment Give I Unto You."
TRINITY CHURCH (now St. Bartholomew's).
Anderson Memorial Window, "He Took Her by the Hand and the Maid Arose."
NORTHMINSTER PRESBYTERIAN CHURCH (destroyed).
Dyer Memorial Window, "Landscape."
ST. JOHN'S MEMORIAL CHURCH.
BOUNDARY AVENUE PRESBYTERIAN CHURCH.
ST. LUKE'S CHURCH.
D'UTASSEY MAUSOLEUM.
Memorial Window, "Christ Child."
ST. JOSEPH'S SEMINARY.
Slattery Memorial Window, "Cross."
WOMEN'S COLLEGE (windows in storage).
Goucher Memorial Window, "Faith, Hope and Charity."
Goucher Memorial Tablet.
McCabe Memorial Window, Ornamental.
Hendricks Memorial Window, Ornamental.
MARYLAND CLUB.
Ornamental Skylight.
HOTEL BELVEDERE.
Ornamental Windows and Skylight.

Catonsville
ST. TIMOTHY'S CHURCH.
James Memorial Window, "St. Michael."
Norman James Window, "Praise."
Farber Memorial Window.
Macgill Memorial Window, "St. Luke."

Centreville
ST. PAUL'S CHURCH.
Ornamental Windows.

Chester Parish, Chestertown
EMMANUEL EPISCOPAL CHURCH.
Westcott Memorial Window, "The Good Shepherd."

Cumberland
EMMANUEL EPISCOPAL CHURCH.
Jefferies Memorial Window, "Second Advent."
Shriver Memorial Window, "The Nativity."
Ornamental Windows.
Decorations.

Ellicott City
ST. JOHN'S EPISCOPAL CHURCH.
Stewart Memorial Window, "Our Saviour."

Hagerstown
ST. JOHN'S LUTHERAN CHURCH.
Mealey Memorial Window, "Charity."
Kausler Memorial Window, "Resurrection."
Mealey Memorial Window, Ornamental.
Rouskulp Memorial Window, "Christ Taking Leave of His Mother."

Ilchester
ST. JOHN'S PROTESTANT EPISCOPAL CHURCH.
Stewart Memorial Window.

Middle River
CHURCH OF THE HOLY COMFORTER
McPherson Memorial Window, "Angel of Light."

Millersville
BALDWIN MEMORIAL CHURCH.
  Woodward Memorial Window, "St. John."

Nottingham
WEST NOTTINGHAM PRESBYTERIAN
CHURCH.
  Gayley Memorial Window, Ornamental.

Salisbury
TRINITY METHODIST EPISCOPAL
CHURCH.
  *Jackson Memorial Window, Mosaic Panel,
  "Their Angels Do Always Behold the Face of
  My Father Which is in Heaven."*

Towson
TRINITY EPISCOPAL CHURCH.
  *Hambleton Memorial Window, "Angel of
  Faith."*

MASSACHUSETTS
Allston
ST. LUKE'S EPISCOPAL CHURCH.
  Mumford Memorial Window, "St. John."

Amherst
MASSACHUSETTS AGRICULTURAL
COLLEGE.
  Dickinson Memorial Tablet.

Andover
MORTUARY CHAPEL.
  *Wood Memorial, Figure and Ornamental
  Windows.*
SOUTH CONGREGATIONAL CHURCH.
  *Shipman Memorial Window, Ornamental.
  Taylor Memorial Window, Ornamental.*

Boston
UNITARIAN CHURCH, (Belmont).
  Atkins Memorial Window, "Guardian Angel."
EMMANUEL EPISCOPAL CHURCH,
  Newbury St.
  *Meyer Memorial Window, "The Incredulity of
  St. Thomas."*
EMMANUEL MISSION CHAPEL.
  *Ornamental Windows.
  Parks Memorial Window, "Epiphany."*
UNITARIAN CHURCH, Warren Street and
  Elm Hill Avenue.
  *Williams Memorial Window, "Angel of
  Resurrection."*
FIRST UNITARIAN CHURCH (combined
  with Second Unitarian).
  Dana Memorial Window.
MT. VERNON CONGREGATIONAL
  CHURCH.
  *Brown Memorial Window, "Resurrection
  Angel."*
NEW OLD SOUTH CHURCH.
  Ornamental Window.
TRINITY CHAPEL.
  Suter Memorial Window.
CENTRAL CONGREGATIONAL
  CHURCH, Berkeley and Newbury Streets
  (now Church of the Covenant).
  *Houghton Memorial Windows, "Abraham
  Leaving Ur," "David and Jonathan" "Joshua
  Before Ai."
  French Memorial Window, "The Resurrection."
  French Memorial Window, "The Nativity."
  Bailey Memorial Window, "Christ at Emmaus."
  Brimbecon Memorial Window, "Christ and the
  Sparrow."
  "L. H." & "M. D. H." Memorial Window,
  "The Four Evangelists."
  Knight Memorial Window, "Miriam."
  Todd Memorial Window, "Dorcas and
  Deborah."
  Russell Memorial Window, "Mary of Bethany."
  French and White Memorial Window,
  "Vision of St. John."
  Memorial Window "The Madonna."
  Grover Memorial Window, "Cornelius and the
  Angel."*

*"S. L. C." Memorial Window, "St.
Augustine and St. Monica."
Ornamental Windows.
Decorations.
Chancel Furniture.
Sanctuary Lamp.*
ARLINGTON STREET CHURCH.
  *Beale Memorial Window, "I Am the Voice."
  Brown Memorial Window, "Annunciation to
  Shepherd."
  Eustis Memorial Window, "Blessed Are the
  Pure in Heart."
  Green Memorial Window, "Blessed Are the
  Meek."
  Greene Memorial Window, "Shepherd."
  Knowles Memorial Window, "Mary at
  Sepulchre."
  Knowles Memorial Window, "Boy Christ in
  Temple."
  Memorial Window, 'Madonna."
  Memorial Window, "Annunciation to Mary."
  Manning Memorial Window, "Prayer in the
  Garden."
  Ornamental Windows.
  Shaw Memorial Window, "Christ Blessing
  Children."
  Wheeler Memorial Window, "Blessed Are the
  Peacemakers."
  Estabrook Memorial 1920.
  Guild Memorial.
  Osgood Memorial.
  Wigglesworth Memorial.*
FIRST BAPTIST CHURCH.
  *Hopkins Memorial Window, "St. John the
  Divine."*
SECOND UNITARIAN CHURCH
  (combined with First Unitarian).
  *Leighton Memorial Window, Mosaic Panel,
  "Truth."
  Lincoln Memorial Tablet.
  Eager Memorial Window, "Mather
  Addressing British Commission."
  Warren Memorial Window, "St. Martin and
  Dorcas."*
TUFTS COLLEGE.
  Pittman Memorial Window, "Easter Lilies."
EQUITABLE BUILDING READING
  ROOM.
  Ornamental Windows.
HOME FOR WANDERERS.
  *Cooper Memorial Window, "Christ Blessing
  Children."*
FOREST HILL CEMETERY.
  Bailey Mausoleum, Landscape.

Brookline
HARVARD STREET CONGREGATIONAL
  CHURCH (burnt down in 1931;
  rededicated in 1933).
  *Reece Memorial Window, "Knowledge."
  Wason Memorial Window, Ornamental.
  Bates Memorial Window, "Faith."
  Hall Memorial Window, "Mary."
  Dwinnell Memorial Window, "Hope."*
ST. PAUL'S EPISCOPAL CHURCH
  (destroyed by fire).
  Candler Memorial Window, Ornamental.
UNITARIAN CONGREGATIONAL
  CHURCH.
  Pastors Memorial Window, Ornamental.
FIRST PARISH UNITARIAN CHURCH.
  Sweetser Memorial Window, "The Nativity."
ST. MARY'S ROMAN CATHOLIC
  CHURCH.
  Morris Memorial Window, Ornamental.
FREE HOSPITAL FOR WOMEN (now the
  Boston Hospital for Women; window
  disappeared in the 1950s).
  *Memorial Window, Ornamental.
  Baker Memorial Window, Landscape.*

Cambridge
NORTH AVENUE CONGREGATIONAL
  CHURCH.
  Ornamental Windows.
OLD CAMBRIDGE BAPTIST CHURCH.
  Ornamental Windows.

PROSPECT STREET CHURCH.
  *Bullard Memorial Window, "Christ Blessing
  Little Children."
  Ornamental Windows.*
SHEPARD MEMORIAL CHURCH (now the
  First Church Congregational).
  *Shepard Guild Window, "The Good Shepherd."
  Horsford Memorial Window, "The Four
  Elements."
  Curtis Memorial Window, "They Shall be
  Mine, Saith the Lord."
  Tilton Memorial Window, "Resurrection
  Angel."
  Ornamental Windows.
  McKenzie Commemoration Window, "Angel."
  Fiske Memorial Window, "St. Catherine of
  Alexandria."
  McKenzie Memorial Window, "Christ Blessing
  Little Children."
  Memorial Window, "Puritan."
  Russell Memorial Window, "St. Paul."
  C. T. Russell Memorial Window, "Faith."
  "Christ and Adoring Angels," Memorial
  Window.*
HARVARD COLLEGE (Memorial Hall).
  *Class of '74, Memorial.
  Class of '61, Memorial.
  Class of '78, Memorial.*
CAMBRIDGE MANUAL TRAINING
  SCHOOL (now the F. H. Rindge Technical
  School).
  Ellis Memorial Tablet.
MUSEUM OF COMPARATIVE
  ZOOLOGY.
  Bronze Tablet.

Dorchester
ST. MARY'S EPISCOPAL CHURCH.
  Bradford Memorial Window, "Christ."

Dudley
CONANT MEMORIAL CHURCH.
  *Conant Memorial Window, "The Peacemakers."
  Ornamental Windows.*

Fitchburg
CHRIST EPISCOPAL CHURCH.
  *Weyman Memorial Window, "The Good
  Shepherd."
  Hastings Memorial Window, "Faith."
  Fay Memorial Windows, "Supper at Emmaus,"
  "Passion Flowers and Grape Vine."
  Crocker Memorial Window, "The
  Resurrection."
  Bartow Memorial Window, "St. Andrew."
  Snow Memorial Window, "Resurrection
  Angel."
  Colony Memorial Window, "Presentation in
  Temple."*
CALVANISTIC CONGREGATIONAL
  CHURCH (now the Faith United Parish).
  *Bailey Memorial Window, "Dorcas."
  Townsend Memorial Window, "Resurrection
  Angel."
  Wallace Memorial Window, "Call of Matthew."
  "Faith."*

Franklin
UNIVERSALIST CHURCH (original building
  destroyed).
  *Hodge Memorial Window, "Isaiah" (window
  missing).*

Groton
PEABODY SCHOOL.
  Potter Memorial Window, "Jacob's Dream."

Hanover
ST. ANDREW'S EPISCOPAL CHURCH.
  *Salmond Memorial Window, "The Good
  Shepherd."
  Sylvester Memorial Window, "Good
  Shepherd."*

Haverhill
FIRST UNIVERSALIST CHURCH.
  Snow Memorial Window, "Christ."

NORTH CONGREGATIONAL CHURCH
(now the First Congregational Church).
Chase Memorial Window, "Madonna."
Seeley Memorial Window, "Ascension."
*Gale Memorial Window, "I Was Hungry and
Ye Gave Me Meat."*
Gardner Memorial Window, "Resurrection."
*Gardner Memorial Window, "Christ in the
Temple."*
*Wood Memorial Window, "Prayer of the
Shepherds."*
*Wentworth Memorial, "Christ and
Nicodemus."*
Carleton Memorial, "The Sower."

Holyoke
CONGREGATIONAL CHURCH.
*Skinner Memorial Window, "Transfiguration"
and Ornamental Skylight.*

Lawrence
**GRACE PROTESTANT EPISCOPAL
CHURCH.**
*Mitchell Memorial Windows, "St. John and the
Annunciation to Mary."*

Lenox
TRINITY CHURCH.
Ornamental Windows.
Arthur Memorial Window.

Longwood
CHURCH OF OUR SAVIOUR.
Lincoln Memorial Window, "Our Saviour."
Lawrence Memorial Window, Ornamental.
Wales Memorial Window, "Resurrection."

Lowell
ST. ANNE'S EPISCOPAL CHURCH.
Parker Memorial Window, "St. Peter."
*Burke Memorial Window, "Resurrection
Morning."*
*Chambre Memorial Window, "Cherubs'
Heads."*
*Cushing Memorial Window, "Ascension, St.
Elizabeth, St. Ann."*
Tweed Memorial Window, "St. Paul."

Manchester
UNITARIAN CHURCH.
*Fitz & Grew Memorial Window, "Resurrection
Angel."*

Melrose
FIRST METHODIST EPISCOPAL CHURCH.
Anderson Memorial Window, "Ascension."

Nantucket
**ST. PAUL'S PROTESTANT EPISCOPAL
CHURCH.**
French Memorial Windows, "Flowers."

New Bedford
**TRINITARIAN CONGREGATIONAL
CHURCH.**
Rugg Memorial Window, "Resurrection Angel."
GRACE EPISCOPAL CHURCH.
*Cammann Memorial Window, "Christ Blessing
Children."*

Newburyport
BAPTIST CHURCH (First Baptist Church).
Bachman Memorial Window, "Benediction."

Newton
ELIOT CONGREGATIONAL CHURCH
(destroyed by fire in the 1950s).
*Coburn Memorial Window, "The Western
Evening Light."*

Newtonville
EMANUEL BAPTIST CHURCH.
Harwood Memorial Window, "King David."
**ST. JOHN'S PROTESTANT EPISCOPAL
CHURCH.**
Hatch Memorial Window, Ornamental.
Webster Memorial Window, "Annunciation."

North Adams
ST. JOHN'S EPISCOPAL CHURCH.
*Averell Memorial Window, "Resurrection
Angel."*
Gatlock Memorial, "St. John."
Wilcoxson Memorial Window, Landscape.
FIRST CONGREGATIONAL CHURCH.
Cady Memorial Window, "St. Luke."
*Hunter Memorial Window, "He Took Her By
the Hand and the Maid Arose."*
*Richardson Memorial Window, "Resurrection
Angel."*
Barber Memorial Window, "Good Shepherd."
Cutting Memorial Window, "Charity."
*Sykes Memorial Window, "Christ Blessing
Little Children."*
Coyle Memorial, "Christ Knocking at the Door."
Wright/Thayer Memorial "The Sower."
Lawrence Memorial, "Hope."
Bubler Memorial, "Resurrection."

North Andover
UNITARIAN CHURCH.
Clark Memorial Tablet.

Northampton
CONGREGATIONAL CHURCH.
James Memorial Window, Landscape.
UNITARIAN CHURCH.
Banister Memorial Window, "Morning Glories."
White Memorial Window, "Autumn Leaves."
SMITH COLLEGE.
Bixler Memorial Window, Ornamental.

Peabody
SOUTH CONGREGATIONAL CHURCH
(Church torn down and windows sold).
Gray Memorial Window, "Good Shepherd."
*Hall Memorial Window, "St. Paul,"
Ornamental and Grape Vine.*
King Memorial Window, "Passion Flower."
Lefavour Memorial Window, "Peace."
*Pevear Memorial Window, "Angel of
Resurrection."*
Pike Memorial Window, "Cross and Lilies."
Thatcher Memorial Window, "Faith."
*Whidden Memorial Windows, "Palm Leaf with
Crown" and Ornamental.*

Pittsfield
ST. STEPHEN'S EPISCOPAL CHURCH.
Smith Memorial Window, "St. Cecilia."
Curtis Memorial Window, "Nativity."
Root Memorial Window, "Angels."
*Kernochan Memorial Window, "Cross and
Doves."*
*Stevens Memorial Window, "Resurrection
Angel."*
CONGREGATIONAL CHURCH (now The
First Church of Christ Congregational).
*Martin Memorial Window, "Angel and
Pilgrims."*

Plymouth
CONGREGATIONAL CHURCH.
*Pilgrims Memorial Window, "Signing the
Compact on the Mayflower."*

Roxbury
FIRST UNIVERSALIST CHURCH.
(torn down in 1960s).
Jenkins Memorial Window, "St. Paul."
*Smith Memorial Window, "Resurrection
Angel."*
Hastings Memorial Window, "Hope."
Morse Memorial Window, "The Madonna."
*James Memorial Window, "The Good
Shepherd."*
*Conant Memorial Window, "Boy Christ in the
Temple."*
*Symbolical Windows, "Passion Flowers" and
"Grape Vine."*
*Pastors Memorial Window, "Christ
Commissioning His Disciples."*
Burrell Memorial Window, "Cross and Lilies."
Curtis Memorial Window, Ornamental.
Colligan Memorial Window, "St. John."
Ornamental Windows.

*Curtis Memorial Window, "Resurrection
Morning."*
Nason Memorial Window, "St. Cecilia."
NEW JERUSALEM CHURCH.
*Robbins Memorial Window, "Mary at the feet of
Jesus."*
**WALNUT AVENUE CONGREGATIONAL
CHURCH** (now The Eliot Congregational
Church).
*Bird Memorial Window, "Resurrection of our
Lord."*
Memorial Window, "Supper at Emmaus."
Ornamental Windows.
*Potter Memorial Window, "Boy Christ in
Temple."*
EMANUEL CHURCH.
Parker Memorial Window, "Resurrection."

Salem
NORTH UNITARIAN CHURCH.
*Willson Memorial Window, "Shepherds
Watching Their Flocks."*
*Peabody Memorial Window, "Faith and
Charity."*
GRACE EPISCOPAL CHURCH.
Endicott Memorial Window.
*Fabens Memorial Window, "St John the
Divine."*
Pitman Memorial Window, "Charity."

Somerville
**WINTER HILL CONGREGATIONAL
CHURCH.**
Woodman Memorial, "The Wise Virgin."
Ornamental Windows.

Southboro
ST. MARK'S EPISCOPAL CHURCH.
Fay Memorial Window, "Gabriel."
PROTESTANT EPISCOPAL CHURCH.
Brown Memorial Window.
ST. MARK'S SCHOOL.
*Thayer Memorial Window, "King Alfred and
Sir Galahad."*

Springfield
CHURCH OF THE UNITY (torn down in the
1960s; windows sold).
*Rumrill Memorial Window, "The Good
Shepherd."*
*Chapin Memorial Window, "Honor thy Father
and Mother."*
*Wesson Memorial Window, "Faith, Hope and
Charity."*
Bliss Memorial Window, "Holy Family."
Warner Memorial Window, "Floral Design."
*Harris Memorial Window, "Lo! I stand at the
door and knock."*
Chapin Memorial Window, "The Holy Night."
Bowles Memorial Window, "Angel of Light."
*Thompson Memorial Window, "Angel of the
Resurrection."*
Memorial Font.
Wolcott Memorial Window, "Come Unto Me."
*Rumrill Memorial Window, "Christ at the
House of Mary and Martha."*
CHRIST (EPISCOPAL) PARISH HOUSE.
Nichols Memorial Window, "Guardian Angel."
MEMORIAL CHURCH PARISH HOUSE.
*Stebbins Memorial Window, "Lilies and
Palms."*
CHESTER CHAPIN CHAPEL.
Memorial Window.
CITY LIBRARY.
Ornamental Windows.
ART MUSEUM.
Ornamental Windows.

Stockbridge
ST. PAUL'S EPISCOPAL CHURCH.
Choate Memorial Window.

Taunton
UNITARIAN CHURCH (now First Parish
Church).
Newbury Memorial Window, "Resurrection."
TRINITARIAN CONGREGATIONAL

CHURCH (now The Pilgrim Congregational Church).
Maltby Memorial Window, "The Good Shepherd."
Isham Memorial Tablet.
Ornamental Windows.
Rhoades Memorial Window, "St. Raphael."

Vineyard Haven
GRACE EPISCOPAL CHURCH.
Cook Memorial Window, "Christ."
Amanx Memorial Window, "Hope."

Wakefield
CONGREGATIONAL CHURCH.
Darling Memorial Window.
FIRST PARISH IN WAKEFIELD.
Ornamental Windows.

Ware
ALL SAINTS ROMAN CATHOLIC CHURCH.
Chancel Windows.
Boyle and Keefe Memorial Windows, "Christ and The Sacred Heart," "SS. Peter and John," "SS. James and Paul," "The Litany."

Watertown
METHODIST CHURCH.
Shaw Memorial Window, "Christ in the Temple."
CHRIST CHURCH.
Storer Memorial Window, "The Nativity."

Wellesley
WELLESLEY COLLEGE.
Scudder Memorial Window, Ornamental (Houghton Chapel).
Houghton Memorial Tablet.
Class of '89, "He Took Her by the Hand and the Maid Arose."
Chaflin Memorial Window, "St. Elizabeth and St. John."
Houghton Memorial Window, "Praise."
Class Window, "Raphael."
Class of '90, '91, '92 Memorials.

West Roxbury
FIRST UNITARIAN CHURCH.
Theodore Parker Memorial Window, "Angel."
Dana Memorial Window, "Guardian Angel."

Weston
UNITARIAN CHURCH.
Gowing Memorial Window, "Resurrection."

Williamstown
ALPHA DELTA PHI HOUSE, WILLIAMS COLLEGE.
Gilbert Memorial Window.
Sanders Memorial Window.
West Memorial Window.
Chamberlin, Goodrich and Hooker Memorial Window.
ST. JOHN'S EPISCOPAL CHURCH.
Huntoon Memorial Window, "St. John."
Leake Memorial Tablet.
Geer Memorial Window, "Boy Christ in Temple."

Winchendon
CHURCH OF THE UNITY.
Damon Memorial Window, "Grape Design."
Solley Memorial Window, "Passion Flowers."

Wollaston
UNITARIAN CONGREGATIONAL CHURCH.
Ornamental Windows.

Worcester
ST. MATTHEW'S EPISCOPAL CHURCH.
Whittall Memorial Window, "Ascension."
Wetmore Memorial Window. "Nativity."
AUDITORIUM OF YOUNG WOMEN'S CHRISTIAN ASSOCIATION.
Ornamental Windows.
ST. MARK'S EPISCOPAL CHURCH.

Center Memorial Window, Ornamental.
ALL SAINTS' CHURCH.
Dewey Memorial Windows.
CENTRAL CONGREGATIONAL CHURCH.
Brownell Memorial Window, "Boy Christ."
ST. PAUL'S CHURCH.
Ornamental Windows.
ST. PETER'S CHURCH.
Ornamental Windows.

Worthington
CONGREGATIONAL CHURCH.
Stone Memorial Window.
Rice Memorial Window.

MEXICO
Mexico City
MEXICAN NATIONAL THEATRE.
Mosaic Curtain.

MICHIGAN
Adrian
CEMETERY.
Arms Mausoleum, "Raphael."

Ann Arbor
UNITARIAN CHURCH.
Lillie Memorial Window, "Angel."
Y. M. C. A. BUILDING.
Fox Memorial Window, Ornamental.

Cross Isle
ST. JAMES CHURCH.
Biddle Memorial Window, "Angel of Praise."

Detroit
WESTMINSTER CHURCH.
Glass Dome.
Decorations.
FIRST PRESBYTERIAN CHURCH.
Pastor's Memorial Window, "St. John."
REFORMED EPISCOPAL CHURCH.
Cummins Memorial Window, "The Good Shepherd."
CASS AVENUE METHODIST CHURCH.
Floral and Ornamental Windows.
JEFFERSON AVE. PRESBYTERIAN CHURCH.
Ornamental Windows.
CEMETERY.
Mausoleum, "Ascension."
ST. JOHN'S PROTESTANT EPISCOPAL CHURCH.
Paine Memorial Window, "St. Agnes."
Prall Memorial Window, "Prayer of Good Shepherd."
Wright Memorial Window, "Christ and Sparrow."
TRINITY CHURCH.
Scott Memorial Window, "Christ Blessing Little Children."
WAYNE COUNTY COURT HOUSE.
Ornamental Windows.

Grand Rapids
PARK AVENUE CONGREGATIONAL CHURCH.
Avery Memorial Window, "The Baptism."
Boise Memorial Window, "Good Shepherd."
Hollister Memorial Window, "Madonna and Child."
Morris Memorial Window, "Angel of Resurrection."
Wallin Memorial Window, "Gethsemane."
White Memorial Window, "Christ at Emmaus."
Withey Memorial Window, "Christ the Comforter."

Hastings
EMMANUEL EPISCOPAL CHURCH.
Wightman Memorial Window, Ornamental.

Jackson
ST. PAUL'S EPISCOPAL CHURCH.

Hayden Memorial Window, "Praise the Lord."

Marquette
ST. PAUL'S CATHEDRAL.
White Memorial Window.
FIRST NATIONAL BANK BUILDING.
Ornamental Dome.
Morgan Memorial Chapel.

Munroe
TRINITY CHURCH.
Story Memorial Window, "Supper at Emmaus."

Saginaw
CEMETERY.
Thompson Mausoleum, Ornamental Window with Cross.
PRESBYTERIAN CHURCH.
Smith Memorial Windows, Ornamental and "Peace."
Stone Memorial Window, "Charity."
ST. JOHN'S EPISCOPAL CHURCH.
Hines Memorial Window, "St. Agnes."

Ypsilanti
STARKWEATHER MEMORIAL CHAPEL.
Ornamental Windows.
FIRST PRESBYTERIAN CHURCH.
Stevens Memorial Window, Ornamental.
STARKWEATHER LIBRARY BUILDING.
Memorial Window.

MINNESOTA
Duluth
FIRST PRESBYTERIAN CHURCH.
Marvin Memorial Window, Ornamental.
Graff Memorial Window, Ornamental.
Rice Memorial Window, Ornamental.
Noble Memorial Window, Ornamental.
Adams Memorial, "Amor, Spes, Felicitas
FIRST BAPTIST CHURCH.
Bilson Memorial Window, "Resurrection."
Steel Memorial Window, "Lilies."
PUBLIC LIBRARY.
Weston Memorial Window, Landscape.
Duluth Memorial, Landscape.
THE PILGRIM CONGREGATIONAL CHURCH.

Fairebault
CONGREGATIONAL CHURCH.
Gale Memorial Window, "At the Tomb."

Minneapolis
CHURCH OF THE REDEEMER.
Rand and Morrison Memorial Window.
Ornamental Windows.
ST. STEPHEN'S ROMAN CATHOLIC CHURCH.
Memorial Window, "The Immaculate Conception."
Memorial Window, "The Good Shepherd."
Memorial Window, "The Sacred Heart."
Memorial Window, "St. Agnes."
Memorial Window, "St. Stephen."
Memorial Window, "St. Patrick."
FIRST CONGREGATIONAL CHURCH.
Ornamental Windows.
Decker Memorial Window, "Angel Holding Scroll."
GETHSEMANE PROTESTANT EPISCOPAL CHURCH.
Peake Memorial Window, Ornamental.
SECOND CHURCH OF CHRIST SCIENTIST.
Kneeland Memorial Window, "Good Shepherd."
WEST PRESBYTERIAN CHURCH (demolished).
McKnight Memorial Window, "Annunciation."
PLYMOUTH CONGREGATIONAL CHURCH.
PUBLIC LIBRARY.
Ornamental Windows.
LAKEWOOD CEMETERY.
Lowery Mausoleum, "A Desert Scout."
THE WEST HOTEL (demolished).

Rochester
CALVARY EPISCOPAL CHURCH.
Graham Memorial Window, "Christ Blessing Little Children."

St. Paul
ST. PAUL'S EPISCOPAL CHURCH.
Perkins Memorial Window, Ornamental.
ST. CLEMENT'S EPISCOPAL CHURCH.
Chancel Window, "Scene on Calvary."
Ornamental Windows.
CENTRAL PRESBYTERIAN CHURCH.
Memorial Window.
ST. PAUL'S CHURCH.
Wright Memorial Window, "Angel."

Stillwater
ASCENSION CHURCH.
Tonnus Memorial Window, "Ascension."
Converse Memorial Window, "Education of the Virgin," "Annunciation to Mary."

Wabasha
GRACE CHURCH.
Irvine Memorial Window, "Three Marys at Tomb."

MISSISSIPPI
Columbus
ST. PAUL'S EPISCOPAL CHURCH.
Cocke Memorial Window, "Resurrection Morning."

Natchez
TRINITY EPISCOPAL CHURCH.
Beltzhoover Memorial Window, "Angel of the Resurrection."
Smith Memorial Window, "Christ Knocking at Door."

University P. O.
UNIVERSITY OF MISSISSIPPI.
Soldiers Memorial Window.

Vicksburg
CHURCH OF THE HOLY TRINITY.
Conway Memorial Window, "Archangel Raphael."
Collier Memorial Window, "Hope."
Martin Memorial Window, "Music."
Smedes Memorial Window, "I Am the Way, the Truth and the Life."
Smith Memorial Window, "Peace."
Norton Memorial Window, "Angel and Field of Lilies."

Yazoo City
TRINITY EPISCOPAL CHURCH.
Duncan Memorial Window, "Moses in the Burning Bush."

MISSOURI
Hannibal
FIRST PRESBYTERIAN CHURCH.
Collins Memorial Window, Ornamental.

Kansas City
TRINITY EPISCOPAL CHURCH.
Chancel Window, "The Last Supper."
Memorial Window.
GRACE EPISCOPAL CHURCH.
Pratt Memorial Window, "Angel of The Nativity."
Berdell Memorial Window, "Angel of the Resurrection."
CHRISTIAN CHURCH.
Long Memorial Window, "Easter Morn."
Rumble Memorial Window, "Parable of the Talents."
CEMETERY.
Mausoleum (Loose), "Angel of Resurrection."
GRAND AVENUE HOTEL.
COATES HOTEL.
MIDLAND HOTEL.

Kirkwood
GRACE EPISCOPAL CHURCH.

Jones Memorial Window, "Except Ye Be As Little Children."

St. Joseph
OWEN MAUSOLEUM.
Ornamental Windows.
FIRST PRESBYTERIAN CHURCH.
Brittain Memorial Window, "Christ Blessing Little Children," and Ornamental Glass.

St. Louis
CONVENT OF THE SACRED HEART.
Altar Windows, "Sacred Heart of Jesus" and "Immaculate Heart of Mary."
ST. PETER'S EPISCOPAL CHURCH (demolished).
Von Wedelstaedt Memorial Window, "Resurrection Angel."
McRee Memorial Window, "Landscape."
Berkeley Memorial Window, "Exodus."
CENTRAL PRESBYTERIAN CHURCH.
Wells Memorial Window, "Charity."
FIRST PRESBYTERIAN CHURCH.
Ornamental Windows.
SECOND PRESBYTERIAN CHURCH.
Breckenridge Memorial Window, "Resurrection."
Cook Memorial Window, "Christ Healing Peter's Wife's Mother."
Copelin Memorial Window, "Ascension."
Guy Memorial Window, "King David."
Herriott Memorial Window, "Faith."
Scott Memorial Window, "John the Baptist."
ST. LOUIS CHURCH.
Clark Memorial Window, "Woman at Well."
FIRST CONGREGATIONAL CHURCH.
Holbrook Memorial Window, "My Peace I Give Unto You."
Patton Memorial Window, "Christ Blessing Little Children."
CEMETERY (Bellefontaine).
Nugent Mausoleum, Landscape (window stolen).
Pierce Mausoleum, "Peace, Salvation, Truth and Understanding."

MONTANA
Billings
BILLINGS MEMORIAL LIBRARY.
Billings Memorial Tablet.

Helena
UNITARIAN CHURCH.
Childs Memorial Window, Ornamental.

NEBRASKA
Falls City
METHODIST CHURCH.
Crow Memorial Window, "Christ and St. John."

Omaha
CHAS. N. DIETZ.
Mausoleum, "A Nile Afterglow," "Prayer in the Desert," "A Desert Scout."

NEW HAMPSHIRE
Amherst
CONGREGATIONAL CHURCH.
Davis Memorial Tablet.

Bretton Woods
STICKNEY MEMORIAL CHAPEL.
Cotton Memorial Window, "St. John."

Charlestown
ST. CATHERINE'S ROMAN CATHOLIC CHURCH.
Birch Memorial Window, Ornamental.
McLean Memorial Window, Ornamental.
Paris Memorial Window, "St. John."

Concord
NEW HAMPSHIRE STATE LIBRARY.
Memorial Tablet.

Dublin
EMMANUEL EPISCOPAL CHURCH.
Parsons's Memorial Window, "Tree of Life."

Hanover
DARTMOUTH COLLEGE, ROLLINS CHAPEL.
Haskell Memorial Tablet.
Stimson Memorial Window, Landscape.

Hopkinton
ST. ANDREW'S PROTESTANT EPISCOPAL CHURCH.
Savory Memorial Window, "St. Andrew."

Keene
UNITARIAN CHURCH (now Unitarian Universalist Church).
Dinsmore Memorial Window, "Truth."

Manchester
WESTMINSTER PRESBYTERIAN CHURCH.
Ornamental Windows.

Rye Beach
ST. ANDREW'S BY THE SEA (Summer Chapel).
Bachelder Memorial Window, Landscape.

NEW JERSEY
Asbury Park
PUBLIC LIBRARY.
Mitchell Memorial Window, Ornamental.

Bay Head
PRESBYTERIAN CHAPEL (now The Bay Head Chapel).
Egbert Memorial Window, Pertaining to Sea.

Bayonne
TRINITY CHURCH.
Brown Memorial Window, Ornamental.

Bloomfield
WESTMINSTER PRESBYTERIAN CHURCH.
Stout Memorial Window, "Resurrection Angel."
Richard Memorial Window, "Presentation in Temple."

Boonton
ST. JOHN'S CHURCH.
Canfield Memorial, "Good Samaritan."

Bound Brook
FIRST PRESBYTERIAN CHURCH.
Brokaw Memorial Window, Ornamental.

Brentwood
PROTESTANT EPISCOPAL CHURCH.
Palmer Memorial Window, Ornamental.

Butler
ST. HUBERT'S CHAPEL.
Kinney Memorial Window, "Symbolic."

Crawford
TRINITY EPISCOPAL CHURCH.
Ornamental Window.

East Orange
BETHEL PRESBYTERIAN CHURCH.
Dodd Memorial Windows, "Faith," "Elijah and the Ravens."
Irving Memorial Window, Ornamental.
GRACE EPISCOPAL PARISH HOUSE.
Broome Memorial Window, "Faith and Hope."

Elberon
ST. JOHN'S EPISCOPAL CHAPEL.
Talbot Memorial Window, Ornamental.
Childs Memorial Tablet.
Hoffman Memorial Tablet.
Drexel Memorial Tablet.
BRIGHTSIDE DAY NURSERY.
Guggenheim Memorial Window, "Charity."

Elizabeth
FIRST PRESBYTERIAN CHURCH.
Dunlap Memorial Window, "Ascension."
Miller Memorial Window, "The Sower."
Thomas Memorial, Medallion, 1924.
Levey Memorial, "Until the Day Break . . ."
ST. JOHN'S EPISCOPAL CHURCH.
Campbell Memorial Window, "Guardian Angel," "Christ" and "Charity."
Lever Memorial Window, "Angel of Resurrection."
TRINITY EPISCOPAL CHURCH.
Howell Memorial Window, "Solomon Instructing Young."
Prenn Memorial Window, "Sermon on the Mount."

Englewood
PRESBYTERIAN CHURCH.
Greene Memorial Window, "The Pilgrim."
McKay Memorial Window, "St. John."
ST. PAUL'S EPISCOPAL CHURCH.
Convers Memorial Window, "Angel of Resurrection."

Flemington
BAPTIST CHURCH.
Higgins and Fluck Memorial Window Ornamental.
Tulper Memorial Window, Ornamental.
PRESBYTERIAN CHURCH.
Broadhead Memorial Window, "Charity and Peace."

Fort Lee
INSTITUTE OF THE HOLY ANGELS.
Sanctuary Dome, "The Holy Spirit."
Ornamental Window.

Glen Ridge
CHRIST CHURCH.
Memorial Window, "Adoration of the Magi."
Memorial Window, "Boy Christ in the Temple" and "The Annunciation."

Greenville
REFORMED CHURCH.
Currie Memorial Window, Ornamental.
Winfield Memorial Window, Ornamental.

Hackensack
SECOND REFORMED CHURCH.
Marshall Memorial Window, "Good Shepherd."
Bogart Memorial Window, "Three Marys at Tomb."
Johnson Memorial Window, "Christ Blessing Children."
Brown Memorial Window, "Angels of the Elements."
Banta Memorial Window, "Annunciation to Mary."
Ornamental Rose Window.
LIBRARY.
Bronze Memorial Tablet.

Hackettstown
CENTENARY COLLEGIATE INSTITUTE.
Hall Bronze Tablet.
Newkirk Peithosophian Hall.

Hoboken
ST. EPISCOPAL CHURCH.
Butts Memorial Window, "The Annunciation."
Brown Memorial Window, "The Ascension."
FIRST PRESBYTERIAN CHURCH.
Griffiths Memorial Window, Ornamental.
Veit Memorial Window, "Gethsemane."

Holmdel
BAPTIST CHURCH.
Ornamental Windows.

Honesdale
Taylor Memorial Window.

Jersey City
PARMLY MEMORIAL BAPTIST CHURCH.

Forster Memorial Window, "Come Unto Me."
ST. JOHN EPISCOPAL CHURCH.
Brixey Memorial Window, "Hope."
Underhill Memorial Window, "Lilies and Palms" and Ornamental, "Poppies and Clematis."
Stratford Memorial Window, "Good Shepherd."

Kinnelon (Butler)
ST. HUBERT'S CHAPEL, ROMAN CATHOLIC.
Jeweled Windows.
Memorial Tablet.
Altar and Altar Furnishings.
Vestments.
Decorations.

Lakewood
ALL SAINT'S EPISCOPAL CHURCH.
Transept Memorial Window, Ornamental.
Kingdon Memorial Window, "Christ Blessing Little Children."
Ornamental Windows.
Mosaic Tablets.
Baptistry Gates.
Y. M. C. A.
McCarty Memorial Tablets.

Lawrenceville
EDITH MEM. CHAPEL (Lawrenceville School).
Boyd Memorial Window, "Easter Morning."
Medallion and Ornamental Windows.

Madison
GRACE EPISCOPAL CHURCH.
Vanderbilt and Twombly Memorial Windows, "Education of the Virgin," "St. Agnes."
Ornamental Windows.
Decorations.
Evans Memorial, "Benedicité," 1913.

Mantolking
EPISCOPAL CHURCH.
Simons Memorial Window, Emblamatic.

Mattawan
PRESBYTERIAN CHURCH.
Ornamental Windows.

Middletown
FIRST CONGREGATIONAL CHURCH.
Hubbard Brass and Wood Tablet.

Millville
PRESBYTERIAN CHURCH.
Mulford Memorial Window, Ornamental.

Montclair
CONGREGATIONAL CHURCH (destroyed by fire in 1917, rebuilt).
Sweet Memorial Window, "St. John the Evangelist."
Inness Memorial Window, "Immortality."
Pinckney Memorial Window, "The Christian Soldier."
Bradford Memorial Window, Ornamental.
Johnson Memorial Window, "Christ Blessing Little Children."
Pray Memorial Window, "Landscape."
FIRST BAPTIST CHURCH.
Harris Memorial Window, "Figure of Christ."
ST. LUKE'S PROTESTANT EPISCOPAL CHURCH.
Ornamental Windows.
TRINITY PRESBYTERIAN CHURCH.
Carlson Memorial Window, Ornamental.
MILITARY ACADEMY.
Bronze Memorial Tablet.

Morristown
ST. PETER'S EPISCOPAL CHURCH.
Transept Window, "St. Peter."
CHURCH OF THE REDEEMER, EPISCOPAL.
Chancel Window, "The Three Marys at the Tomb."

PRESBYTERIAN CHURCH.
Stone Memorial Window, "The Good Shepherd."
Spedden Memorial Window, "Resurrection."

Mount Holly
TRINITY EPISCOPAL CHURCH.
Byllesby Memorial Window, Ornamental.

Newark
DUTCH REFORMED CHURCH (Belleville).
McDonald Memorial Window, "Presentation in the Temple."
PEDDIE MEMORIAL CHURCH.
Ornamental Windows.
NORTH REFORMED CHURCH.
Ornamental Windows.
FIRST CONGREGATIONAL CHURCH.
Frelinghuysen Memorial Window.
WICKLIFFE PRESBYTERIAN CHURCH.
Brinsmade Memorial Window, "St. John."
FIFTH AVENUE PRESBYTERIAN CHURCH.
Ward Memorial Window, "Angel of Faith."
HOUSE OF PRAYER.
Williams Memorial Window, "St. Genevieve and St. Germain."
ST. PAUL'S EPISCOPAL CHURCH.
Barlow Memorial Window, "Mary Kneeling at the Feet of Jesus."
Ornamental Windows.
TRINITY EPISCOPAL CHURCH.
Colton Memorial Window, "The Pilgrims."
MT. PLEASANT CEMETERY.
Odell Mausoleum, Memorial Window, "Angel of Peace."

New Brunswick
FIRST REFORMED CHURCH.
Voorhees Memorial Window, "The Pilgrims."
Lettson Memorial Window, "Our Lord and St. Mary."
CHRIST EPISCOPAL CHURCH.
Parker Memorial Window, "Annunciation."
KIRKPATRICK MEMORIAL CHAPEL.
Titsworth Memorial Window, Ornamental.
RUTGERS COLLEGE.
Class of 1901, Ornamental.
Ornamental Windows.
MAUSOLEUM.
Johnson, "Landscape."

Norwood
CHURCH OF THE HOLY COMMUNION, EPISCOPAL.
Oakley Memorial Window, "The Resurrection of Christ."

Oceanic (now Rumson)
PRESBYTERIAN CHURCH.
Ornamental Windows.

Orange
GRACE CHURCH.
Barstow Memorial Window, "Easter Morning."
HILLSIDE PRESBYTERIAN CHURCH.
Memorial Window, "Christ Blessing Little Children."
Van Gaasbeck Bronze Tablet.
Carter Memorial Tablet.
CONGREGATIONAL CHURCH.
Dotger Memorial Window, "Faith."
FIRST UNITARIAN CHURCH.
Hunt Memorial Window, Ornamental.
GRACE EPISCOPAL CHURCH.
Hathaway Memorial Window, "Angels" "The Four Evangelists."
ORANGE VALLEY CHURCH.
Sunday School Memorial Window, "Christ."

Passaic
FIRST PRESBYTERIAN CHURCH.
Fish Memorial Window, "The Good Shepherd."
Barry Memorial Window, "Prophesying Michael."
Memorial Window, "Christ on Road to Emmaus."

Paterson
CHURCH OF THE REDEEMER,
  PRESBYTERIAN (now The Church of the
  Messiah, Presbyterian).
  Hornblower Memorial Window.
ST. PAUL'S EPISCOPAL CHURCH.
  Hall Memorial Window, "The Ascension."
  *Marsh Memorial Window, "The River of the
  Water of Life."*
  *Collet Memorial Window, "Angel of
  Adoration."*
  McFarlan Hymn Boards.
  *Dodge Memorial Window, "Landscape and
  Cherubs' Heads."*
  *Hutchinson Memorial Window, "I am the
  Resurrection and the Life."*
  *Hall Memorial Window, "Angel of
  Resurrection."*
  *Newton Memorial Window, "An Adaptation of
  Gozzoli."*
  Symbolic Windows.
FIRST PRESBYTERIAN CHURCH.
  Hobart Memorial Window, "Good Shepherd."
ST. MARY'S CHURCH.
  Ornamental Windows.
HAMILTON TRUST COMPANY.
  Ornamental Dome.

Perth Amboy
ST. PETER'S EPISCOPAL CHURCH.
  Newport Memorial Window, "Our Saviour."

Plainfield
CRESCENT AVENUE PRESBYTERIAN
  CHURCH.
  Ornamental Window.
GRACE CHURCH.
  Tweedy Memorial Window.
  Ornamental Window.

Princeton
MARQUAND CHAPEL (destroyed by fire in
  1920).
  *Garrett Memorial Window, "St. John and
  Divine."*
PRINCETON METHODIST EPIS.
  CHURCH.
  Durell Memorial Window, "St. George."
ALEXANDER COMMENCEMENT HALL.
  Ornamental Windows.
  *Rose Window, "Knowledge, Fame, Genius,
  Study."*
  *Mosaic Panels, "The Heroes and Heroines of the
  Homeric Story."*
TIGER INN CLUB.
  Ornamental Windows.

Ridgewood
METHODIST EPISCOPAL CHURCH.
  *Phillip's Memorial Window, "The Soul is
  Risen."*
REFORMED CHURCH.
  LaFetra Memorial Window, "Symbolic."

Rutherford
FIRST PRESBYTERIAN CHURCH.
  *Dean Memorial Window, "The Virtuous
  Woman."*
GRACE EPISCOPAL CHURCH.
  Bain Memorial Window, Ornamental.

Salem
FIRST PRESBYTERIAN CHURCH.
  Sheron Memorial Window, Ornamental.
ST. JOHN'S CHURCH.
  *Sinnickson Memorial Window, "Light of the
  World."*

Somerset
CHAPEL OF WASHINGTONVILLE.
  Ornamental Windows.

Somerville
ST. JOHN'S EPISCOPAL CHURCH.
  Smith Memorial Window, "The Resurrection."
  Potts Memorial Window, Landscape.
  Greenleaf Memorial Window, Landscape.
  Parmelee Memorial Window, "Charity."

  *Schott Memorial Window, "Christ Blessing
  Children."*
FIRST REFORMED CHURCH.
  Case Memorial Window, Ornamental.
  Vincent Memorial Window, Ornamental.
  Memorial Tablet.

South Orange
CHURCH OF THE HOLY COMMUNION.
  *Hoskier Memorial Window, "Return from
  Calvary."*
  Thierior Memorial Window, Ornamental.
  *Barstow Memorial Window, "Good
  Shepherd."*

Summit
CALVARY EPISCOPAL CHURCH..
  Poor Memorial Window, "The Beatitudes."
  Ornamental Windows.

Trenton
METHODIST CHURCH, State Street.
  *Isaac Wood Memorial Window, "The Good
  Shepherd."*
  *William Wood Memorial Window, "Christ
  Knocking at the Door."*

NORTH CAROLINA
Brevard
ST. PHILIP'S EPISCOPAL CHURCH.
  *Breese Memorial Window, "Hospitality and
  Charity."*

Charlotte
SECOND PRESBYTERIAN CHURCH.
  Memorial Window.
ST. PETER'S EPISCOPAL CHURCH.
  Smith Memorial Window, "Angel of Faith."

Edenton
CALVARY EPISCOPAL CHURCH.
  Wood Memorial Window, "Moses."

Hillsboro
ST. MATTHEW'S EPISCOPAL CHURCH.
  Ruffin Memorial Window, "Angel of Praise."

Raleigh
FIRST PRESBYTERIAN CHURCH.
  Inman Memorial Window, Ornamental.

OHIO
Akron
CEMETERY.
  Robinson Mausoleum, "Good Shepherd."

Cadiz
FIRST PRESBYTERIAN CHURCH.
  *Dewey Memorial Window, Ornamental and
  "Resurrection."*

Cedarville
REFORMED PRESBYTERIAN CHURCH.
  Reid Memorial Window.

Cincinnati
CALVARY PRESBYTERIAN CHURCH
  (Clifton).
  Miller Memorial Window, "Faith."
  Schoenberger Memorial Window, "Angel."
  *Schoenberger Memorial Window, "The Last
  Supper."*
  Neave Memorial Window.
  Andrews Memorial Window, "The Baptism."
  Law Memorial Window, Landscape.
  Schoonmaker Memorial Window, "Resurrection."
CHURCH OF THE ADVENT, EPISCOPAL,
  (Walnut Hill).
  Bates Memorial Window, "Angel of Faith."
CHRIST EPISCOPAL CHURCH.
  Ornamental Windows.
  Decorations.
  Hanging Lamps.
CHURCH OF OUR SAVIOUR.
  Groesbeck Memorial Window, "Our Saviour."
CHRIST CHURCH.

  *Memorial Windows, "Angel Choir" and
  "St. Andrew Bringing Brother to Christ."*
CHURCH OF THE NATIVITY.
  Marrow Memorial Window.
COURT HOUSE.
CHURCH OF NEW JERUSALEM (Church
  demolished; windows removed).
  *Lawson Memorial Window, "Christ on Road to
  Emmaus."*
  *Memorial Window, "Angels Representing
  Seven Churches."*
FIRST CONGREGATIONAL CHURCH.
  Thompson Memorial Window, "Truth."
GRACE PROTESTANT EPISCOPAL
  CHURCH (now St. Michael's and All
  Angels).
  Blake Memorial Tablet.
  Magill Memorial Window, "Angel of Faith."
  *Mitchell Memorial Window, "Resurrection
  Angel."*
MT. AUBURN PRESBYTERIAN CHURCH.
  Addy Memorial Window.
  McAlpine Memorial Window.

Cleveland
EUCLID AVENUE BAPTIST CHURCH.
  Chisholm Memorial Window, "The Crusader."
  Hurlburt Memorial Window, "Head of Christ."
EUCLID AVENUE PRESBYTERIAN
  CHURCH.
  Beckwith Memorial Window.
ST. PAUL'S EPISCOPAL CHURCH.
  King Memorial Window, "The Resurrection."
  Scott Memorial Window, "Cherubim."
  *Bolton Memorial Windows, Ornamental,
  "Raising of Lazarus," "Christ and Nicodemus."*
  Gibbs Memorial Window, "Woman of Samaria."
  *Norton-Bolton Memorial Window, "Angel
  Bearing Message of God."*
  Memorial Window, Angel Heads.
  *Memorial Window, "St Paul Preaching at
  Athens" and "The Raising of Jarius' Daughter."*
SECOND PRESBYTERIAN CHURCH.
  Baldwin Memorial Window, "The Holy Spirit."
  Hurlburt Memorial Window, "Our Saviour."
CHURCH OF THE UNITY (4 windows sold,
  4 stolen).
  *Everitte Memorial Window, "Angel of
  Resurrection."*
  Upson Memorial Window, "Recording Angel."
  Wason Memorial Window, "Angel of Victory."
CALVARY PRESBYTERIAN CHURCH.
  *Bingham Memorial Window, "Angel of
  Resurrection."*
  Memorial Window.
  Ornamental Windows.
BECKWITH MEMORIAL CHURCH.
BELLFLOWER AVENUE MEMORIAL
  CHURCH.
  Severence Memorial Window, Ornamental.
FIRST CONGREGATIONAL CHURCH.
  Ornamental Windows.
GRACE EPISCOPAL CHURCH.
  *Widlar Memorial Window, "Blessed Are
  the Pure in Heart."*
ROCKEFELLER BUILDING.
  Ornamental Skylights.
ADELBERT COLLEGE.
  Pope Memorial Tablet.
CLEVELAND ART SCHOOL.
  Ornamental Window.
LAKEVIEW CEMETERY.
  *Andrews Mausoleum, "In My Father's House
  Are Many Mansions" and "Sir Galahad."*
  Beach Mausoleum, Window.
  Kirk Mausoleum, "St. Cecilia."
  Raine Mausoleum, "Angel of Record."
  Moore Mausoleum, Lily Treatment.
WADE MEMORIAL CHAPEL.
  Wade Memorial Window, Ornamental.

Chillicothe
FIRST PRESBYTERIAN CHURCH
  destroyed by fire in 1956).
  Carlisle Memorial Window, "Angels of Praise."
  *Fullerton Memorial Window, "Angel of the
  Resurrection."*
  Nipgen Memorial Window, "Cross and Lilies."

Brown Memorial Window, "Grape Vine."
Franklin Memorial Window, "Palm Leaves."
Dun Memorial Window, "The Resurrection."
Worthington Memorial Window, Ornamental.
Massey Memorial Window, "The Holy Spirit."
Patterson Memorial Window, "Floral Design."
Cochran Memorial Window, Ornamental.
Martha Memorial Window, Ornamental.
Ornamental Windows.

Clifton
CHRIST CHURCH.

Columbus
THE BROAD STREET PRESBYTERIAN
CHURCH, Broad Street and Garfield
Avenue.
Green Memorial Window, "The Resurrection."
Sharp Memorial Window, "Angel of Hope."
Taylor Memorial Window, "Angel of Victory."
Nichols Memorial Window, "St. John."
Ornamental Windows.
Goodspeed Memorial Window, "Christ
Blessing Little Children."
MORTUARY CHAPEL.
Huntington Memorial Window.
COLUMBUS CLUB.
McKinley Memorial Tablet.

Dayton
FIRST PRESBYTERIAN CHURCH.
Van Ausdal Memorial Window, "Adoring
Angel."
FIRST BAPTIST CHURCH.
Ornamental Windows.
WOODLAWN CEMETERY.
Low Mausoleum, "Vision of Holy City."

Delaware
ASBURY METHODIST EPISCOPAL
CHURCH.
Ornamental Windows.

Elyria
FIRST CONGREGATIONAL CHURCH.
Beebe Memorial Window, "Come Unto Me."
Memorial Windows, "Three Marys,"
"Nativity," "Christ Blessing Children" and
Ornamental.

Glendale
CHRIST EPISCOPAL CHURCH.
Hodge Memorial Window, Ornamental.

Greenfield
FIRST METHODIST CHURCH.
Baldwin Memorial Window, "King David."
McLain Memorial Window, "Annunciation."
Memorial Window, "Eastern Morn."
Ornamental Windows.

Hamilton
WESTMINSTER PRESBYTERIAN
CHURCH.
Falconer Memorial Window, "The Sower."
LUTHERAN CHURCH.
Benninghofen Memorial Window,
"Resurrection."

Marion
FIRST PRESBYTERIAN CHURCH.
Fisher Memorial Window, Landscape.

Massillon
ST. TIMOTHY'S PROTESTANT EPIS.
CHURCH.
Gates Memorial Window, Landscape.

Newark
TRINITY EPISCOPAL CHURCH.
Quincy Memorial Window, "Ascension."

Painesville
CHAPEL, LAKE ERIE COLLEGE (destroyed
by fire in 1950).
Evans Memorial Window, "Angel of
Resurrection."
Storrs Memorial Window, "Motherhood and
Music."

Steubenville
ST. PAUL'S CHURCH.
Means Memorial Window, "Christ the
Comforter" and "Angel of Resurrection."
ST. STEPHEN'S CHURCH.
Elliott Memorial Window, "The Sower."
ELLIOTT MAUSOLEUM.
Ornamental Window.

Toledo
FIRST CONGREGATIONAL CHURCH.
Emerson Memorial, "Moses."
Eaton Memorial Window.
Carrington Memorial Window.
Casey Memorial Window.
Wood Memorial Window.
Williams Memorial Tablet.
Bowman Memorial Tablet.
Bowman Memorial Window, Ornamental.
Williams Memorial, "Christ Blessing Little
Child."
Nearing Memorial Window, Landscape.
ST. PAUL'S METHODIST EPISCOPAL
CHURCH.
Commandary Memorial Window, Emblematic.

Warren
CHRIST EPISCOPAL CHURCH.
Morgan Memorial Window, "Guardian Angel,"
"Angel of Adoration."
Kinsman Memorial Window, "Come Unto
Me."

Youngstown
FIRST PRESBYTERIAN CHURCH.
Baldwin Memorial Window, "Three Marys at
the Tomb" and "Christ Blessing Children."
ST. JOHN'S PROTESTANT EPISCOPAL
CHURCH.
Botsford Memorial Window, "Angel of
Resurrection."
Tod-Arrell Window, "Te Deum."

Zanesville
FIRST PRESBYTERIAN CHURCH.
Wills Memorial Window, Ornamental.
PUTMAN PRESBYTERIAN CHURCH.
Jewett Memorial Window, "Return of the Soul."

PENNSYLVANIA
Allegheny
CALVARY METHODIST CHURCH.
Horne Memorial Window, "The Ascension."
Shea Memorial Window, "The Resurrection."
Simpson Memorial Window, "The Apocalypse."
NORTH PRESBYTERIAN CHURCH.
Reymer Memorial Window, "Angel of Peace."
EMMANUEL EPISCOPAL CHURCH.
Hay Memorial Window, Ornamental.
ALLEGHENY CEMETERY CHAPEL.
Ornamental Windows.
ST. PAUL'S PROTESTANT EPISCOPAL
CHURCH.
Painter Memorial Window, "St. John on Isle of
Patmus."
CEMETERY.
Schreimer Mausoleum, Ornamental.

Altoona
ST. LUKE'S EPISCOPAL CHURCH.
Reed Memorial Window, "Mary at Tomb."

Andalusia
ALL SAINT'S CHURCH.
King Memorial Window.

Andmore
ST. MARY'S EPISCOPAL CHURCH.
Harrison Memorial Window, "Annunciation
and Adoring Angels."

Ashbourne
ST. PAUL'S EPISCOPAL CHURCH.
Widener Memorial Window, "The Resurrection."
Fox Memorial Window, "Te Deum."
Tyler Memorial Window, "Behold I stand at the
Door and Knock."

Bala
CHURCH OF ST. ASAPH, EPISCOPAL.
Roberts Memorial Window, Ornamental.

Bedford
ST. JAMES EPISCOPAL CHURCH.
Lyon Memorial Window Ornamental.

Bethlehem
METHODIST EPISCOPAL CHURCH.
Linderman Memorial Window, "Figure of
Christ."

Birdsboro
ST. MICHAEL'S CHURCH.

Blue Ridge Summit
CALVARY MISSION.
Rich Memorial Window, "Calvary."

Brownsville
CHRIST EPISCOPAL CHURCH.
Clark Memorial Window, Ornamental.
Dawson & Patterson Memorial Window
Ornamental.

Bryn Mawr
BRYN MAWR PRESBYTERIAN CHURCH.
Hensel Memorial Window, "Good Shepherd."
Johnson Memorial Window, "St. John the
Divine."
Converse Memorial Window, "St. Agnes."
Snowden Memorial Window, "Landscape."

Canonsburg
FIRST PRESBYTERIAN CHURCH.
Ornamental Windows.

Carbondale
TRINITY CHURCH.
Law Memorial Window, "Angel of
Resurrection."

Carlisle
ST. PATRICK'S ROMAN CATHOLIC
CHURCH.
Gable Window, "Emblems of the Evangelists."

Chambersburg
PRESBYTERIAN CHURCH.
Nixon Memorial Window, "Angel of Faith."
CENTRAL PRESBYTERIAN CHURCH.
Cree Memorial Window, "Good Shepherd."
Ornamental Windows.
Sherrard Memorial Window, "I Am the Way,
the Truth and the Life."
FALLING SPRING CHURCH.
Crawford Memorial Window, "Good Shepherd."
WILSON COLLEGE.
Edgar Memorial Window, "Instruction."

Charlottesville
CHRIST EPISCOPAL CHURCH.
Stone Memorial Window, Ornamental.

Chester
ST. PAUL'S CHURCH.
Tate Memorial Window, "Nativity."

Clayville
PRESBYTERIAN CHURCH.
Hogue Memorial Tablet.

Cornwells
ST. CHARLES ROMAN CATHOLIC
CHURCH.
Drexel Memorial Window, "Angels."

Downington
ST. JAMES' CHURCH.
McIlvaine Memorial Window, Ornamental.
Park Memorial Window, Ornamental.

Doylestown
ST. PAUL'S LUTHERN CHURCH.
Mann Memorial Window, "Come unto Me."

Drifton
ST. JAMES EPISCOPAL CHURCH.
Coxe Memorial Window, "The Lord is My Shepherd."

Eaglesmere
ST. JOHN IN WILDERNESS.
Clay Memorial Window, "Easter Morning."
Emery Memorial Window, "Te Deum."

Easton
BRAINERD UNION PRESBYTERIAN CHURCH.
Seibert Memorial Window, Ornamental.
LAFAYETTE COLLEGE.
Coffin Memorial Tablet (destroyed by fire).
Van Winckle Memorial Window, "Death of Sir Philip Sidney."
Warfield Memorial Window, "Alquin and Charlemagne."

Elkins Park
ST. PAUL'S CHURCH.
Eastman Memorial Window, "Paul Preaching at Athens."

Erie
ST. PAUL'S EPISCOPAL CHURCH.
Metcalf Memorial Window, Ornamental.
FIRST PRESBYTERIAN CHURCH.
Selden Memorial Window, "The Good Shepherd."
FIRST PRESBYTERIAN CHURCH.
Ornamental Windows.
Schoonmaker Memorial Window, "St. John."
Shannon Memorial Window, Ornamental.

Franklin
ST. JOHN'S EPISCOPAL CHURCH.
Lewis Memorial Tablet.
Baum Memorial Window, "Landscape and St. Agnes."
Brydon Memorial Window, "Resurrection."
Hayes Memorial Window, "Christ Blessing Children."
McCalmont Memorial Window, "Finding Boy Christ in the Temple."
Plumer Memorial Window, "The Shepherd," "St. Michael," "Angels of Praise," "Angel and Cherubs' Heads."
Aigner Memorial Window, "Christ and Four Evangelists."
Lewis Memorial Window, Ornamental.

Germantown
CALVARY PROTESTANT EPISCOPAL CHURCH.
Perry Memorial Window, "Disputation."
Memorial Window, "Flight Into Egypt."
FIRST METHODIST EPISCOPAL CHURCH.
Billings Memorial Window, "Annunciation to Shepherds."
Epworth League Memorial Window, "Boy Christ in Temple."
Funnell Memorial Window, "St. Luke" and "St. John."
Parker Memorial Window, "Sermon on the Mount."
Roop Memorial Window, "St. Matthew."
Shelmerdine Memorial Window, "St. Mark" and "Nativity."
Smyth Memorial Window, "Ascension."
Memorial Window, "Resurrection Morning."
Bodine Memorial Window, "Christ Blessing Little Children."
FIRST PRESBYTERIAN CHURCH.
Bayard Henry Memorial Window, "Ascension," "Light of World," "Victory and Peace."
Charles W. Henry Memorial Window, "They Shall Receive a Crown of Glory" and Ornamental Rose Window.
ST. MICHAEL'S EPISCOPAL CHURCH.
Dunn Memorial Window, "Temperance."
Lloyd Memorial Window, "Education of Virgin."
ST. PETER'S CHURCH.
Statesbury, "Cornelius and Angel."

SECOND PRESBYTERIAN CHURCH.
Elliott Memorial Window, "The Sower."
Kimball Memorial Window, "The Sacrifice."
SUMMIT PRESBYTERIAN CHURCH.
McCown Memorial Window, "Angel of Peace" and Ornamental.
CEMETERY.
Warden Mausoleum, "Figure of Christ."

Hamburg
FIRST REFORMED CHURCH.
Deer Memorial Window, "Passion Flowers."

Hanover
EMANUEL CHURCH.
Forney Memorial Window, "Come Unto Me."

Harrisburg
PRESBYTERIAN CHURCH.
Reynolds Memorial Window, "Faith."
GRACE METHODIST EPISCOPAL CHURCH.
Beggs Memorial Window, "Ascension."
MARKET SQUARE PRESBYTERIAN CHURCH.
Hickok Memorial Window, "Ascension."

Haverford
CHURCH OF THE REDEEMER.
Cassatt Memorial Window, "Education of Virgin" and "Saint Agnes."

Hazelton
ST. JOSEPH'S CHAPEL.
Ornamental Windows.

Holmesburg
EMANUEL CHURCH.
Wilson Memorial Window, "Figure of Christ."

Honesdale
GRACE EPISCOPAL CHURCH.
Gunn Memorial Window.
Thompson Memorial Window.
Dimmick Memorial, "I Am the Way, the Truth and the Life."

Ithan
ST. MARTIN'S CHAPEL.
Stroud Memorial Window, Ornamental.

Kingston
PRESBYTERIAN CHURCH.
Teter Memorial Window, "Christ Blessing Children."

Kittaning
PRESBYTERIAN CHURCH.
Dull Memorial Window, "Faith."
Mayers Memorial Window.
Colwell Memorial Window.
Brown Memorial Window.
Ewing Memorial Window.
Phillips Memorial Window.
Painter Memorial Window.
Ornamental Windows.

Lancaster
ST. JAMES EPISCOPAL CHURCH.
Reynolds Memorial Window, "Angel of the Resurrection."
Nauman Memorial Window, "Angel of Praise."
FIRST PRESBYTERIAN CHURCH.
Mitchell Memorial Window, "Come Unto Me."

Lewiston
LEWISTON METHODIST EPISCOPAL CHURCH.
Pitcairne Memorial Window, "Ascension."
ST. MARK'S EPISCOPAL CHURCH.
Norris Memorial Window, "St. Michael."
Culbertson Memorial Window, "Last Supper."

Lock Haven
ST. PAUL'S EPISCOPAL CHURCH.
Beardsley Memorial Window, "St. John the Evangelist."

Mauch Chunk
FIRST PRESBYTERIAN CHURCH.
Leisenring Memorial Window, "The Ascension."
ST. MARK'S EPISCOPAL CHURCH.
Butler Memorial Window, "Abide with us."

Mercersburg
MERCERSBURG ACADEMY.
Ornamental Windows.

Montrose
ST. PAUL'S EPISCOPAL CHURCH.
Sayre Memorial Window, "Raphael."

Muncy
ST. JAMES' CHURCH.
Ornamental Window.

Newcastle
TRINITY CHURCH.
Ohl Memorial Windows, "Resurrection Morning" and "Charity."

New London
PRESBYTERIAN CHURCH.
Strawbridge Memorial Window, "Good Shepherd."

Overbrook
MEMORIAL CHURCH OF ST. PAUL.
Scott Memorial Windows, "Angel of Peace" and "Angel of Resurrection."

Palmerton
ST. JOHN'S CHURCH.
Hardenberg Memorial Window, "Behold the Lamb of God."

Philadelphia
CHRIST CHURCH CHAPEL, EPISCOPAL, 20th and Pine Streets.
Thayer Memorial Window, "St. John the Evangelist."
Hart Memorial Window, "Our Saviour."
Nixon Memorial Window, "Dorcas."
Ornamental Windows.
CHURCH OF THE HOLY TRINITY, EPISCOPAL, 19th and Walnut Streets.
Miller Memorial Window, "Angel."
Coffin Memorial Window, "Moses and the Law."
Ebbs Memorial Window, "Adoration of the Cross."
Godfrey Memorial Window, "Soldier of the Cross."
Milne Memorial Window, "Light of the World."
CHURCH OF THE MEDIATOR, EPISCOPAL, 19th and Lombard Streets.
Everitt Memorial Window, "Angel and Lilies."
Norris Memorial Window, "Cross, Vine and Passion Flowers."
Joseph Hughes Memorial Window, "St. Paul."
Ellen Hughes Memorial Window, "Lo! I Stand at the Door and Knock."
Wirgman Memorial Window, "Resurrection Angel."
ST. LUKE'S EPISCOPAL CHURCH, (Germantown).
Upjohn Memorial Window, "Angel."
McCullagh Memorial Window, "Archangel."
CALVARY EPISCOPAL CHURCH, (Germantown).
Stevens Memorial Window, "Mt. Calvary."
Ingersoll Memorial Window, "Mary at the Tomb."
Henry Memorial Window, "The Visit of the Magi."
Conrad Memorial Window, "Abraham Offering Isaac."
Potter Memorial Window, "The Brazen Serpent."
GRACE EPISCOPAL CHURCH, (Mt. Airy, Germantown).
Carstairs Memorial Window, Ornamental.

ST. JAMES EPISCOPAL CHURCH, 22nd and Walnut Streets.
Graham Memorial Window, "The Good Shepherd."
Cox Memorial Window, "Adoring Angel."
Grover Memorial Window, "Gloria in Excelsis Deo."
Smith Memorial Windows, "Annunciation," "Education of Virgin" and "St. Agnes."
CHAPEL OF THE HOLY COMMUNION, EPISCOPAL, 27th and Wharton Streets.
Thomas Memorial Window, "Communion of the Saints."
Thomas Memorial Window, "The Benediction."
CHURCH OF THE SAVIOUR, EPISCOPAL, 38th and Arch Streets.
Williams Memorial Window, "Christ Healing Peter's Wife's Mother."
CALVARY EPISCOPAL CHURCH, 41st Street.
Kennedy Memorial Window, Ornamental.
TRINITY EPISCOPAL CHURCH, (Oxford Church P. O.).
Memorial Window, "Christ the Consoler."
Whitaker Memorial Window.
ST. PHILIP'S EPISCOPAL CHURCH, 42nd Street and Baltimore Avenue.
Thomas Memorial Window.
ST. ANDREW'S EPISCOPAL CHURCH, 38th and Baring Streets.
McIlvaine Memorial Window, "Meeting of Elizabeth and Mary."
Chancel Memorial Window, Ornamental.
Chancel Decorations.
Powell Memorial Window, "Resurrection."
EMMANUEL EPISCOPAL CHURCH, (Holmesburg).
Bourns Memorial Window, "Our Saviour."
NORTHMINSTER PRESBYTERIAN CHURCH, 35th and Baring Streets.
Ogelsby Memorial Window, "Come Unto Me."
Andrews Memorial Window, Ornamental.
NORTH BROAD STREET PRESBYTERIAN CHURCH, Broad and Green Streets.
Dr. Harper Memorial Window, "Christ in the Temple."
Stewart Memorial Window, "Moses."
Hogg Memorial Window, "Angel of Peace."
Belfield Memorial Window, "St. Matthew."
Kemble Memorial Window, "St. Mark."
Potter Memorial Window, "St. Luke."
Sweatnam Memorial Window, "St. John."
Young Memorial Window, Ornamental.
Johns Memorial Window, Ornamental.
Schenck Memorial Window, Ornamental.
Hoar Memorial Window, Ornamental.
Grier Memorial Window, Ornamental.
Hand Memorial Window, Ornamental.
Marsh Memorial Window, Ornamental.
Martin Memorial Window, Ornamental.
Dr. John Stites Memorial Window, Ornamental.
Whillden Memorial Window, Ornamental.
Alex. Willden Memorial Window, Ornamental.
Wood Memorial Window, Ornamental.
Ornamental Windows.
FIRST PRESBYTERIAN CHURCH, (Germantown).
Henry Memorial Window, "Rebecca at the Well."
HOLLAND MEMORIAL CHURCH, Federal and Broad Streets.
Memorial Windows, "St. Mark," "St. Matthew," "St. Luke."
Morris Memorial Window, "St. John."
Five Windows: "I was an hungered, and ye gave me to eat."
"I was thirsty, and ye gave me drink."
"I was a stranger, and ye took me in."
"I was naked, and ye clothed me."
"I was sick, and ye visited me."
COLUMBIA AVENUE PRESBYTERIAN CHURCH, 21st Street and Columbia Avenue.
Three Gable Windows: "An Angel," "Our

Saviour," "The Disputation in the Temple."
Ornamental Windows.
FIRST UNITARIAN CHURCH.
Bartol Memorial Window, "Blessed are the Pure in Heart."
LEE AVENUE BAPTIST CHURCH.
Ornamental Windows.
WARDEN MAUSOLEUM, (Germantown).
Memorial Window, "Christ the Consoler."
CALVARY METHODIST EPISCOPAL CHURCH.
May Memorial Window, "Resurrection."
Memorial Window, "Ascension."
CALVARY PRESBYTERIAN CHURCH.
Converse Memorial Window, "The Sower."
Lewis Memorial Window, "The Angelic Choir."
Hubbell Memorial Window, "Ruth and Naomi."
CHURCH OF OUR SAVIOUR.
Biddle Memorial Window, "The Baptism."
FIRST UNITARIAN CHURCH.
Lewis Memorial Window, Ornamental.
HOWARD MEMORIAL CHURCH.
Memorial Windows, Symbols of Twelve Apostles, and Ornamental Windows.
ST. LUKE'S EPISCOPAL CHURCH.
Bradley Memorial Window, "St. Elizabeth of Hungary."
ST. MARTIN'S IN THE FIELDS (WISSAHICKON).
Henry Memorial Window, "St. Martin."
Houghton Memorial Window, "Christ Blessing Children."
Smith Memorial Window, "St. Augustine" and "St. Monica."
Houston Memorial Tablet.
ST. MATTHEW EPISCOPAL CHURCH.
Powell Memorial Window, "Boy David."
ST. PAUL'S PRESBYTERIAN CHURCH.
Wanamaker Memorial Window, Ornamental.
ST. PAUL'S EPISCOPAL CHURCH.
Glending Memorial Window, "Madonna and Child."
Ornamental Windows.
ST. PETER'S CHURCH.
Vibbert Memorial Window, "Elizabeth of Hungary."
ST. STEPHEN'S CHURCH.
Widener Memorial Window, "Come Unto Me."
SECOND PRESBYTERIAN CHURCH.
Logan Memorial Windows, "Abraham, Samuel, Joseph, Moses, Elijah, Isaiah, Daniel."
TABERNACLE PRESBYTERIAN CHURCH.
Perkins Memorial Window, "Faith and Hope."
McCook Memorial Window, "Valiant Woman."
TENTH PRESBYTERIAN CHURCH.
Gordon Memorial Window, "Coat of Arms of Presbyterian Church."
Patterson Memorial Window, "Resurrection Angel."
ROMAN CATHOLIC PROTECTORY.
Barry Memorial Window, "Holy Family."
EPISCOPAL ACADEMY.
Benson Memorial Window, "St. George."
HORTICULTURAL HALL.
Ornamental Window.
NEW PHILADELPHIA HIGH SCHOOL.
Steel Memorial Window, "Education."
AMERICAN BAPTIST PUBLISHING SOCIETY.
Ornamental Windows.
UNION LEAGUE CLUB.
WEST LAUREL HILL CEMETERY.
Burk Mausoleum, "Come Unto Me."
Hughes Mausoleum, "Angel of Resurrection."
Powell Mausoleum, "Gethsamane."
Curran Mausoleum, "Towards a Better World."
Baine Mausoleum, "Faith."
Carter Mausoleum, "Light of the World."
Kenworthy Mausoleum, "Christ Knocking at the Door."
Rorke Mausoleum, "St. John the Devine."
Williams Mausoleum, "Boy Christ in Temple."
Ziegler Mausoleum, Landscape.
Meshert Mausoleum, Coat of Arms.
NORTH LAUREL HILL CEMETERY.
Parish Mausoleum, Landscape.
SOUTH LAUREL HILL CEMETERY.

Forderer Mausoleum, Egyptian.
LAUREL HILL CEMETERY.
Stehle Mausoleum, "I Am the Way, the Truth and the Life."
Schinzel Mausoleum, Ornamental.
Widener Mausoleum, "In My Father's House Are Many Mansions."
WESTMINSTER CEMETERY.
Markley Mausoleum, "Seated Angel."

Pittsburgh
CHRIST METHODIST CHURCH.
Horne Memorial Window, "The Sermon on the Mount."
Holmes Memorial Window, "Marriage of Cana."
Memorial Window, "Christ Charge to His Disciples."
ST. PETER'S EPISCOPAL CHURCH.
Carter Memorial Window.
CALVARY EPISCOPAL CHURCH.
Chancel Window, "Christ the Consoler."
FIRST EVANGELICAL LUTHERAN CHURCH.
Black Memorial Window, "Christ and Glorifying Angels."
FIRST PRESBYTERIAN CHURCH.
Paxton Memorial Window, "The Sower."
Chalfont Memorial Window, "Good Samaritan and Angel of Charity."
Dalzell Memorial Window, "The Nativity."
Davidson Memorial Window, "The Good Shepherd" and "Angel of Life."
Denney Memorial Windows, "Easter Morn" and "Resurrection."
Hayes Memorial Window, "Ascension."
Miss Carry Hayes Memorial Window, "Vision of Holy City and Adoring Angels."
Herron Memorial Windows, "Christ Preaching" and "Prophet Isaiah."
Kepler Memorial, "Christ, Faith, Hope and Charity."
Laughlin-Phillips Memorial Window, "Christ Blessing Little Children."
Purves Memorial Window, "Call of Matthew," and "St. John the Baptist."
Robinson Memorial Windows, "Annunciation to Mary" and "Angels of Peace and Hope."
Speer Memorial Windows, "Annunciation to Shepherds" and "Angels of Salvation."
Ornamental Windows.
SHADYSIDE PRESBYTERIAN CHURCH.
Beatty Memorial Window, "The Nativity."
ST. ANDREW'S PROTESTANT EPIS. CHURCH.
DuPuy Memorial Window, "Christ Blessing Little Children."
THIRD PRESBYTERIAN CHURCH.
Albree Memorial Window, "Angels of Praise."
Bushnell Memorial Window, "Sacrifice of Isaac."
Edwards Memorial Window, "Gabriel and Purity and Peace."
Laughlin Memorial Window, "Star of Bethlehem."
Schwartz Memorial Window, "The Prophets."
Shaw Memorial Window, "Christ and Nicodemus."
Thaw Memorial Window, "The Holy City."
Chandler Memorial Window, Ornamental.
DU QUESNE BANK.

Pittston
ST. JAMES CHURCH.
Jones Memorial Window, "Te Deum."

Pottstown
CHURCH OF THE TRANSFIGURATION.
Rittenhouse & Evans Memorial Window, Ornamental.

Pottsville
FIRST PRESBYTERIAN CHURCH.
Kaercher Memorial Window, "Angel of the Resurrection."
TRINITY EPISCOPAL CHURCH.
Atkins Memorial Window, "Gethsemane."

Reading
CHRIST CHURCH CATHEDRAL.

221

Stichner Memorial Window.
ST. BARNABAS CHURCH.
Ornamental Window.
TRINITY LUTHERAN CHURCH.
Miller Memorial Window, Ornamental.
Dauth Memorial Window, "Charity."
Harbster Memorial Window, "Martin Luther."
Arnold Memorial Window, "Our Saviour."
Seitzinger Memorial Window, "St. Paul."
Henry A. Muhlenberg Memorial Window,
"Faith."
Heister A. Muhlenberg Memorial Window,
"Hope."
Rightmeyer Memorial Window, Ornamental.
Otto Memorial Window, Ornamental.
Fry Testimonial Window, "The Good
Shepherd."
Ornamental Windows.

Scranton
ST. LUKE'S EPISCOPAL CHURCH.
Memorial Window, "The Ascension."
CHURCH OF HOLY ROSARY.
McManus Memorial Window, Ornamental.
FIRST PRESBYTERIAN CHURCH.
Platt Memorial Window, "Ascension."
NEW UNIVERSALIST CHURCH.
Payne Memorial Window, "Faith."
SECOND PRESBYTERIAN CHURCH.
Gearhart Memorial Window, "Charity."
Henshaw Memorial Window, "Angel of Faith."
ST. LUKE'S CHURCH.
Dickson Memorial Window, "The Nativity."
CEMETERY.
Simpson Memorial Window, "Lilies."
Jermyn Mausoleum, "Angel."

Sewickley
ST. STEPHEN'S EPISCOPAL CHURCH.
Young Memorial Window.
FIRST PRESBYTERIAN CHURCH.
Nevin Memorial Window, "Good Shepherd."
Shannon Memorial Window, "Madonna and
Child."
Travelli Memorial Window, "Good
Samaritan."
Davis Memorial Window, "St. Cecelia."
Robinson Memorial Window, "St. Peter."
Rutan Memorial Window, "Paul Preaching at
Athens."
Shannon Memorial Window, "Faith."
Nevin Memorial Window, "Hope."
Woods Memorial Window, "Charity."

Shamokin
FIRST PRESBYTERIAN CHURCH.
Ornamental Windows.

Sharon
Buhl Mausoleum, Ornamental.

Steelton
CEMETERY.
Crumbler Mausoleum.

Torresdale
ALL SAINTS' CHURCH.
King Memorial Window, "Ascension."

Uniontown
PRESBYTERIAN CHURCH.
Memorial Windows: "The Nativity."
"The Adoration of the
Shepherd."
"Madonna and Child."
"The Disputation."
"Christ Blessing Little
Children."
"The Resurrection."
"The Ascension."
Ornamental Windows.
ST. PETER'S EPISCOPAL CHURCH
Howell Memorial Window, "Meeting in the
Garden."

Wayne
ST. MARY'S MEMORIAL CHURCH.

Rolin Memorial Window, "Good Shepherd."
Gosling Memorial Window, "Boy David."

Wellsboro
ST. PAUL'S PROTESTANT EPISCOPAL
CHURCH.
Siemens Memorial Window, Ornamental.

Westchester
HOLY TRINITY EPISCOPAL CHURCH.
Townsend Memorial Window, "Angels."
Norris Memorial Window, "Adoration of the
Cross."
FIRST PRESBYTERIAN CHURCH.
Pinkerton Memorial Window, "The Child
Christ."

White Marsh
ST. THOMAS' EPISCOPAL CHURCH.
Van Rennsaelaer Memorial Window, "Angel of
Faith."

Wilkesbarre
PRESBYTERIAN CHURCH.
Hodge Memorial Window, "Resurrection Angel."
Ornamental Windows.
ST. STEPHEN'S EPISCOPAL CHURCH.
Jones Memorial Window.
FIRST PRESBYTERIAN CHURCH.
Miller Memorial Window, "Herald Angels."
Flick Memorial Window, "Figure of Truth."
McClintock Memorial Window, "Prayer of
Shepherd."

Williamsport
CHRIST EPISCOPAL CHURCH.
Brown Memorial Window, "Ascension."
Munson Memorial Window, "Nativity."
White Memorial Window, "Good Shepherd."
CHURCH OF THE COVENANT
(Presbyterian).
Brown Memorial Window.
CEMETERY.
Munson Mausoleum, "Angel of Resurrection."
McCormick Mausoleum, Ornamental.
CHURCH OF ANNUNCIATION.
Costello Memorial Window, "Ascension."

Wyncote
ALL HALLOW'S EPISCOPAL CHURCH.
Altar and Reredos.
Chancel Furniture.
Sanctuary Rail.
Sanctuary Lamp.
Curtiss Memorial Window.
PRESBYTERIAN CHURCH.
Sharpless Memorial Window, Ornamental.

York
CEMETERY.
LaFean Mausoleum, Ornamental.

RHODE ISLAND
Barrington
ST. JOHN'S CHURCH.
Chapin Memorial Window, "King's
Daughters" (disappeared).

Bristol
ST. MICHAEL'S EPISCOPAL CHURCH.
Howe Memorial Window, "St. Michael."

E. Greenwich
ST. LUKE'S EPISCOPAL CHURCH.
Goddard Memorial Window, Landscape.

Jamestown
ST. MATTHEW'S EPISCOPAL CHURCH.
Clark Memorial Windows, "Raphael" and
"Resurrection Angel."

Narragansett Pier
ST. PETER'S EPISCOPAL CHURCH.
Minton Memorial Window, "Peace."
McGowan Memorial Window, "Angel of
Resurrection."

Newport
BELMONT MEMORIAL CHAPEL.
Belmont Memorial Window, "St Elizabeth of
Hungary."
BERKELEY MEMORIAL CHAPEL.
TRINITY EPISCOPAL CHURCH.
Stewart Memorial Window, "Valiant Woman."
Burden Memorial Windows.
Ornamental Windows.
Vanderbilt Memorial, "St. Michael."
Y. M. C. A.
Vanderbilt Cast Bronze Tablet.

Providence
CENTRAL BAPTIST CHURCH.
Hartwell Memorial, Landscape, 1917.
CONVENT OF THE SACRED HEART,
Elmhurst (torn down circa 1970).
Memorial Windows: "Adoring Angels."
"The Incredulity of St.
Thomas."
"The Agony in the
Garden."
"The First Communion of
St. Aloysius."
"Christ Blessing Little
Children."
"Baptism of Our Lord."
"The Nativity."
"The Flight into Egypt."
"The Disputation."
"St. John the Evangelist."
"Rabboni."
Ornamental Windows.
Decorations.
Altars and Altar Furniture.
Episcopal Chair and Prie-Dieu.
Sanctuary Lamps.
Stations of the Cross.
Memorial Tablet.
Mural Paintings: "The Annunciation."
"The Visitation."
GRACE EPISCOPAL CHURCH.
Memorial Window.
ST. STEPHEN'S EPISCOPAL CHURCH.
Seagrave Memorial Windows, "The Guardian
Angel," "The Good Shepherd."
Bajnotti Memorial Window, "The Angel of
Consolation."
CALVARY BAPTIST CHURCH.
Memorial Windows, "St. Andrew," "Faith"
and Ornamental.
ST. JOHN'S EPISCOPAL CHURCH.
Goddard Memorial Window, "Christ and Call
to Matthew."
ABELL MAUSOLEUM.
Memorial Window, "Among the Vines."

Wakefield
CHURCH OF THE ASCENSION.
Woodward Memorial Window, "Valiant
Woman."
Updike Memorial.
Randolph Memorial.

Westerly
COTTRELL MAUSOLEUM.
Memorial Window, "Angel of Faith."

SOUTH CAROLINA
Charlestown
ST. MICHAEL'S EPISCOPAL CHURCH.
Frost Memorial Window, "St. Michael."
Andrew Simons Memorial Window, "Easter
Morning."
John Simons Memorial Window, "Annunciation
to Virgin."
TRINITY METHODIST EPISCOPAL
CHURCH.
Williams Memorial Window, "Come Unto
Me."

SOUTH DAKOTA
Sioux Falls
ALL SAINTS' SCHOOL
Natwick Memorial Window, "Angel of
Resurrection."

TENNESSEE
Chattanooga
CHURCH OF ST. PETER AND ST. PAUL.
Memorial Window, "Scenes from Life of St. Peter and St. Paul."

Dyersburgh
PRESBYTERIAN CHURCH.
Parr Memorial Window, "Madonna."
Latta Memorial Window.

Knoxville
FIRST PRESBYTERIAN CHURCH.
Barker Memorial Window, Ornamental.
Vanuxern Memorial Window, "Angels of Praise."

Maryville
MARYVILLE COLLEGE.
Ornamental Window.

Memphis
GRACE CHURCH.
Gage Memorial Window, "Ascension."

Nashville
CHRIST EPISCOPAL CHURCH.
Warner Memorial Window, "Home at Nazareth."
FIRST METHODIST CHURCH.
Memorial Windows, "Moses, St. Paul, David," and Ornamental.
PRESBYTERIAN CHURCH.
Overton Memorial Window, "I Am the Way, Truth and Life."

TEXAS
Dallas
CHRIST CHURCH CATHEDRAL.
Belo Memorial Window, "St. John, Moses and St. Paul."

Denison
FIRST CONGREGATIONAL CHURCH.
Ornamental Windows.

Galveston
TRINITY EPISCOPAL CHURCH.
Bird Memorial Window, "The Guardian Angel."
FIRST PRESBYTERIAN CHURCH.
Perry Memorial Window, "The Good Shepherd."
League Memorial Window, "Peace."
TRINITY EPISCOPAL CHURCH.
Sealy Memorial Window, "Suffer Little Children to Come Unto Me."

Houston
EPISCOPAL CHURCH.
Belo Memorial Window, "Charity."

UTAH
Salt Lake City
TEMPLE OF THE LATTER DAY SAINTS.
Memorial Windows, A Series of Historical Subjects.
Ornamental Windows.
ST. MARK'S CATHEDRAL.
Leonard Memorial Window, "Reaper."
Norris Memorial Window, "Incidents from Life of St. Mark."

VERMONT
Barton
CONGREGATIONAL CHURCH.
Kimball Memorial Window, "The Ascension."

Brandon
RITCHIE MEMORIAL EPISCOPAL CHURCH.
Harrison and Gittings Memorial Window.

Brattleboro
FIRST BAPTIST CHURCH.

Fuller Memorial Window, "St. John the Divine."

Burlington
ST. PAUL'S EPISCOPAL CHURCH.
Weaver Memorial Window, Ornamental.

Montpelier
EPISCOPAL CHURCH.
Moss Memorial Window.

Proctor
CHURCH OF THE UNITY.
Proctor Memorial Windows, Landscape (three).

St. Albans
FIRST CONGREGATIONAL CHURCH.
Smith Memorial Window, Landscape.
Smith Memorial Window, "Peace."

Shelbourne Falls
TRINITY EPISCOPAL CHURCH (formerly Trinity Mission Church).
Vanderbilt and Webb Memorial Window, "Our Saviour."
Chittenden and Clap Memorial Windows, "Baptism" and "Last Supper."
Ornamental Windows.

Vernon
UNION CHURCH.
Wood Memorial Window, "Disputation in Temple."

Woodstock
CHURCH OF ST. JAMES THE GREAT, EPISCOPAL.
Clapp Memorial Window, "St. James the Great."
PRESBYTERIAN CHURCH.
Ornamental Windows.
CONGREGATIONAL CHURCH.
Billings Memorial Window, Ornamental.

VIRGINIA
Charlottesville
CHRIST CHURCH.
Morehant Memorial Window, Ornamental.
Dold Memorial Window, "St. Cecelia."
Page Memorial Window, Ornamental.
Stone Memorial Window, Ornamental.
Wood Memorial Window, "Resurrection Angel."
UNIVERSITY OF VIRGINIA.
Moore Memorial Window, Ornamental.
Thornton Memorial Window, "St. Luke."
Ornamental Windows.

Fortress Monroe
CHAPEL OF THE CENTURION, EPISCOPAL.
Squire Memorial Window.
McAllister Memorial Window.

Fredricksburgh
PRESBYTERIAN CHURCH.
French Memorial Window, "The Good Shepherd."

Leesburg
ST. JAMES PROTESTANT EPISCOPAL CHURCH.
Smith Memorial Windows, Ornamental, "Cross and Lilies."

Manchester
PRESBYTERIAN CHURCH.
Hall Memorial.

Norfolk
ST. LUKE'S EPISCOPAL CHURCH.
Taliaferro Memorial Window, "Our Lord as Prophet, Priest and King."
ST. PAUL'S CHURCH.
Bonsell Memorial Window, "Three Marys at Tomb."

Petersburg
BLANDFORD MORTUARY CHAPEL.
State of South Carolina, "St. Mark."
Tennessee, "St. Philip."
Alabama, "St. Andrew."
Mississippi, "St. James."
Missouri, "St. Peter."
Virginia, "St. John."
Washington Art. Corps, "St. Paul."
North Carolina, "St. Bartholomew."
Ornamental Windows.

Portsmouth
ST. JOHN'S EPISCOPAL CHURCH.
Watts Memorial Window, "Come Unto Me."
TRINITY EPISCOPAL.
Crocker Memorial Window, "Resurrection."
Martaugh Memorial Window, Ornamental.
Reed Memorial Window, "Angel."

Richmond
ST. PAUL'S EPISCOPAL CHURCH.
Anderson Memorial Window, "Christ Blessing Little Children."
Blair Memorial Window, "The Pilgrims."
Mosaic Reredos, Anderson Memorial, "The Last supper."
Smelling Memorial Window, "Angel of Hope."
Ross Memorial Window, "Paul Before Agrippa."
Newton Memorial Window, "Annunciation."
Jefferson Davis Memorial.
SECOND PRESBYTERIAN CHURCH.
Hawes Memorial Window, "Dorcas."
CHURCH OF HOLY TRINITY.
Warwick Memorial Window, "Angel."
MONUMENTAL PROTESTANT EPIS. CHURCH.
Newton Memorial Window, "Ascension."
CONFEDERATE MUSEUM.
Poe Memorial Window, "Spirit of Confederacy."
ALL SAINTS' EPISCOPAL CHURCH.
Whitcomb Memorial Window, "The Beatitudes."
Saunders Memorial Window, "Resurrection."
Mayo Memorial Window, "Te Deum" and Ornamental.
Freedly Memorial Window, "Christ Blessing Children."
GRACE ST. PRESBYTERIAN CHURCH.
Memorial Window.

Rockbridge Baths
BETHESDA CHAPEL.
Miller Memorial Window, Ornamental.

Staunton
TRINITY EPISCOPAL CHURCH.
Taylor Memorial Window, "St. Luke."
Bell Memorial Window, "Ascension."
Catlett Memorial Window, "Easter Morn."
Walter Memorial Window, "Faith and the Good Samaritan."
Miller Memorial, Landscape.
(plus 8 other windows).

Tappanhannock
ST. JOHN'S EPISCOPAL CHURCH.
McGuire Memorial Window, Ornamental.

WEST VIRGINIA
Charleston
ST. JOHN'S CHURCH.
Roller Memorial Window, "Taken from Life of St. John."
KANAWHA PRESBYTERIAN CHURCH.
Smith Memorial Window, Landscape.

Clarksburg
CHRIST EPISCOPAL CHURCH.
Lowndes Memorial Window, "I Am the Way, Truth and Life."

Huntington
TRINITY EPISCOPAL CHURCH.
Huntington Memorial Window, "Good Shepherd."

Kanawha
KANAWHA PRESBYTERIAN CHURCH.
Arter Memorial Window, "The Lord is My Shepherd."

Mont de Chantel
MONASTERY OF VISITATION.
Robertson Memorial Windows, "Sacred Heart," "Margaret and Mary," "St. Francis de Sales," "St. Eulalia," "St. Agnes," "St. Cecelia," "St. James," "Good Shepherd," "St. Francis de Chantel."

Wheeling
WHEELING HOSPITAL.
Howell & Hubbard Memorial Tablets.
ST. MATTHEW EPISCOPAL CHURCH.
Brady Memorial Window, "Resurrection Angel."
Halloway Memorial Window, "Presentation in Temple."
Milton Memorial Window, "Angel of Peace."
Oglebay Memorial Window, "Christ Knocking at Door."
Scott Memorial Window, "Peace."
Peterson Memorial.

WISCONSIN
Appleton
GRACE EPISCOPAL CHURCH.
Reid Memorial Window, "Dorcas."

Kenosha
CONGREGATIONAL CHURCH.
Hoyt Memorial Window, "Cornelius and Angel."
Newell Memorial Window, "Christ and Charity."

La Crosse
CHRIST EPISCOPAL CHURCH.
Cameron Memorial Window, "Figure of Christ."

Madison
GRACE CHURCH.
Proudfit Memorial Window, "Christ Blessing Children."
FIRST BAPTIST CHURCH.
Spooner Memorial Window, "Good Shepherd."

Milwaukee
ST. PAUL'S EPISCOPAL CHURCH.
Kemper Memorial Window, "Christ Leaving the Praetorium."
Colt Memorial Window, "Resurrection Angel."
Miller Memorial Window, "Stars of Bethlehem."
FIRST BAPTIST CHURCH.
Colly Memorial Window, Ornamental.
Roundy Memorial Window, "I Am the Way, Truth and Life."
IMMANUEL PRESBYTERIAN CHURCH.
Merrill Memorial Window, "Christ Blessing Children."
Young Memorial Window, "Praise and Peace."
Goodrich and Van Dyke Memorial Window, "Angel of Resurrection."
PLYMOUTH PRESBYTERIAN CHURCH.
Stark Memorial Window, Ornamental.
ALL SAINTS' CATHEDRAL SCHOOL CHAPEL.
Bosworth Memorial Window, "Guardian Angel."
WOMEN'S CLUB.
Field Memorial Window, Ornamental.

Oshkosh
TRINITY EPISCOPAL CHURCH.
Barber Memorial Window, "Angel of Prayer."

SOUTH AUSTRALIA
Adelaide
ST. PAUL'S CHURCH.
Ayer Memorial Windows, "Faith" and Landscape.

SCOTLAND
Dunfermline
ABBEY, Music Hall.
Carnegie Memorial, Landscape.

Edinburgh
ST. CUTHBERT'S CHURCH.
East Memorial Window, Landscape with Figure.

Killin
MEMORIAL HALL.
Todd Memorial Window, Ornamental.

Tyvie
TYVIE CHURCH.
Forbes-Leith Memorial Window, "St. Michael."

ENGLAND
Kimbolton
KIMBOLTON CHURCH.
Duchess of Manchester Memorial Window, "Christ Blessing Children."

London
NEW COLLEGE CHAPEL.
East Memorial Window, Landscape.

FRANCE
Paris
AMERICAN CHURCH.
Wanamaker Memorial Window, "Faith and Love."

HAWAIIAN ISLANDS
Honolulu
ST. ELIZABETH CHAPEL.
Proctor Memorial Window, "St. Elizabeth."
Castle Memorial, Medallion Rose Window.
CHURCH HALL OF HAMAKUA MILL CO.
Davies Memorial Window, "Cross."

CANADA
London, Ontario
ST. PAUL'S CATHEDRAL, EPISCOPAL.
Meredith Memorial Window, "The Good Shepherd."

Montreal
AMERICAN PRESBYTERIAN CHURCH.
Lyman Memorial Window, "Christ at Emmaus."
Cheney Memorial Window, "The Good Shepherd."
Nelson Memorial Window, "Angel of Praise."
Cassills Memorial Window, "Faith."
Ross Memorial Window, "St. Paul."
Green Memorial Window, "Come Unto Me."
Hayes Memorial Window, "Charity."
McWilliams Memorial Window, "Christ Blessing Children."
Hastings Memorial Window, "Faith."
Nelson Memorial Window, "Cornelius and Angel."
Green Memorial Window, "Angel of Resurrection."
Holton Memorial Window, "Hope."
Childs Memorial Window, "Nativity."
Cassils Memorial Window, "St. Agnes, Shepherd, Madonna and Child."